Patty A Wilson

Where Dead Men Walk Vol. I

By:

Patty A. Wilson

Where Dead Men Walk
Vol. I

Have you ever glimpsed something from the corner of your eye--but you were alone?

Have you ever thought that someone was calling your name--but no one else was home?

In this book you'll read stories from ordinary folks who had extraordinary experiences.

You'll read of a young Sharon Tate who spent the night in her boyfriend's home only to see a ghastly vision that would become reality only later.

You'll visit Fairacres in Canada and learn of the strange, twisted history of this lovely property.

You'll read about a woman who purchased an inn in Van Buren, Arkansas and who found that though she lives there by herself, she is not alone.

You'll read about a young man who was on patrol in France during World War II. He was intent upon surviving to return home, but one night he found himself following a spirit...

You'll read about a man who had a strange experience in a small English village when a legend became fact before his very eyes.

You'll read about a Mexican high school that is haunted by a singer from the building's time as a nightclub.

You'll visit one of the most haunted sites in Australia and experience the ghosts the way tourists and staff have.

I won't say more now. I'll allow you to begin your journey of haunted homes, inns and hotels. I'll welcome you into a world where reality suddenly fades away leaving you struggling with what you see, feel or hear... I'll welcome you to my world, and I hope that you will survive this world of shadow without too much fear... Of course, some fear can be fun, so off you go to begin your journey. Welcome to a land Where Dead Men Walk...

Where Dead Men Walk Vol. I
Copyright (c) 2001, Patty A. Wilson

ISBN: 0-9700650-2-7

Cover design by John Evanko

All rights reserved. No part of this book, either in part or in whole, may be reproduced, transmitted or utilized in any form or by any means, electronic, photographic, or mechanical, including photocopying, recording, or by any information storage and retrieval system, without the permission in writing from the Publisher, except for brief quotations embodied in literary articles and reviews.

First Printing: August 2001

For permission, or for serialization, condensation, or for adaptions, write the Publisher at the address below:

Piney Creek Press
P.O. Box 227
Roaring Spring, PA 16673
(814) 793-2260
pineycrk@pennswoods.net

Before You Begin Reading:

Though I have tried to use the real names of people in the following stories, there are a few times when it has been requested that I use pseudonyms. When they appear, they will be printed as follows: *Terry Smith.

DEDICATION

This book is dedicated to my sons who were extremely patient while I chained myself to the computer. Thanks for your help, patience and love, Daniel, Michael and Benjamin. I hope you know that you are always first in my book!

To Mom who made me work hard, and to Terry who always believed in my dreams.

And to Scott, my best friend, who has traveled a road he never imagined. Hope you're enjoying the journey.

ACKNOWLEDGMENTS

In order to complete such a book I had to rely upon the help and patience of many people whom I'd like to thank now. Thanks to Jackie Henningsen of the Van Buren Inn, Mr. Douglas Prindle, Gerald Reed and his daughter Teri Garza, and the many other folks who write to me. I truly appreciate your letters and I am grateful for your trust. A special thanks to Richard Crowe of Chicago Supernatural Tours. His help with the Oprah Winfrey story was invaluable in clearing up some historical errors. To Eileen Luz Johnston of the Bernardsville Library, thank you so much for your help. Without your wonderful book and all of your help, I could not have told the story of Phyllis to the world.

I appreciate the many businesses where the management made time for me, such as those who own and/or manage the Crescent Hotel, the Mansions, and the Van Buren Inn. Thank you.

Thanks, also, to the wonderful research staffs at the many government organizations I contacted for verifications. Your help and timely responses are greatly appreciated. If I missed anyone else who contributed to this book, forgive me. I assure you that it was not intentional.

I'd also like to thank a special friend who spent last winter proofreading this book. Scott, your patience and ability to share my vision are amazing. Thanks, my friend.

Patty Wilson

AUTHOR'S NOTE

Dear Reader,

I've been honored to bring to you a sampling of the many stories of ghosts, hauntings and visitations from around the world. In the thirty-four stories to follow you will find many intriguing tales. Some are stories which you might think you are familiar with; but I assure you that I've pieced together some interesting information about them. Other stories, such as The Haunted Van Buren Inn, have never been told before in a major book. I hope that you are intrigued, entertained and a little frightened by the true stories you're about to read.

I began my journey in this field by chronicling ghost stories, but I soon realized that it would not be enough. I realized that I'd have to truly "research" them and experience a haunting for myself if possible. With that in mind, my friends Al Brindza and Scott Crownover began the Paranormal Research Foundation with me. We attempt to apply science to this field, strangely called parapsychology. In future volumes I hope to report upon sites we have actually spent time researching in, but for now I hope you'll enjoy the true stories I have collected from around the world.

If you have a true story you'd like to share, please write to me at the address below. I'd love to hear your story and perhaps it might appear in another book.

Patty A. Wilson
August 2001

Patty A. Wilson

Patty A. Wilson
PO Box 227
Roaring Spring, PA 16673

TABLE OF CONTENTS

The Haunted Van Buren Inn	1
Sharon Tate's Ghostly Warning	10
The Spirits Of Quarantine Station, Australia	13
The Ghostly Kitten	18
Leigh Masters And Sam	20
The Haunted Crescent Hotel	23
The Patrol	29
The Many Haunts of Heathrow	32
The Curse Aboard the Titanic	34
Stone Cold Spirits	40
The Red Girl Of Huntington College	46
What Will Happen To Phyllis Parker?	47
Black Jake And The Delta Saloon	59
Sunnyland	60
The Sounds From Hell	61
What Haunts The Mansions Hotel?	68
The Hobo	74
From Beyond The Grave	77
San Antonio's Lost Children	79
The Crying Girl	82
"Play For Me, Beth."	85
The Hauntings at Berlin's Old Palace	87
The Haunted High School of Tijuana	92
The Mansion Called Fairacres	93
The Haunted Oprah Studio	96
President Lincoln and the Rathbone Curse	99
The Ghost of Gillian's Way	107
The Best Little Restaurant	110
The Last Good-bye	113
Nelly Butler's Return	115
The Voices	124
The Willow Saloon	127
The Haunted Studio	131
Childer's Night	133
Bibliography	137

THE HAUNTED VAN BUREN INN

The lot at 7th and Main in Van Buren, Arkansas is now the home of the historic and classic Van Buren Inn, but the lot has a long history. In 1840 the lot was granted to a private citizen by President Van Buren. A building was constructed but it burned down prior to 1882. The history of this first building is sketchy at best, but in 1882 a new building was started on the site. This building was to be a bank. It took seven years to build the Crawford County Bank, but it was worth the wait. The building was considered one of the most advanced buildings of its time. It was an unique blend of architecture which, though beautiful, has almost never been copied. The bank was built primarily of red brick, but with its turrets and peeks it looked more like a whimsical fairyland castle than the functional bank it was.

Eventually the bank was closed and the building went through various periods of use. At one time it housed a community hall, a speakeasy and was the site of at least one murder. Various other businesses were run from the building, but eventually it was left to molder.

Through the years of neglect this care in design and choice of materials saved the building from dereliction. It was long abandoned but the charm remained in tact until it caught the eye of a woman named Jackie Henningsen from California. Jackie fell in love with the building, saw its potential, and she bought it. It was a major undertaking which required an unbelievable commitment on her part. She moved her family to Van Buren, Arkansas in 1989 and began the long task of rescuing the building.

Jackie, her daughter and a young man who had worked for her in California worked on the repairs themselves. As she needed new skills, Jackie learned them herself and her dedication paid off. Jackie created a beautiful inn where local folks can enjoy fine food at her restaurant and visitors may come to experience her unique brand of down home charm and old-time elegance. Jackie's very nature puts a person immediately at ease and at least a good part of the charm of the inn comes from Jackie's own personality.

Soon after purchasing the building back in 1988 Jackie realized that someone or something else was sharing the building with her. Jackie moved into the building in January of 1989 and began working on the remodeling. She had brought along a young man who had worked for her in California. The young fellow often made jokes about the "ghost." He told Jackie that he always felt as if someone was on his heels, in his body space. He also felt pushed. Time after time, the young man would suddenly spin around while walking down the second floor hall to catch the person, but no one was there. After that they tried to ignore the spirit; no one wanted to admit that the spirit was real.

Jackie and her hired help felt uncomfortable in the building, especially in the second floor hallway. They tried to explain away the uneasy feeling by attributing it to the terrible neglect of the building and the fact that they could not turn on any lights. The building was literally rotting in places and it had a terrible, musty smell. The electrical inspector had banned them from using any electricity until the ancient, fire-prone, cloth-covered wiring could be replaced.

Jackie said, "...not one of us wanted to walk the 2nd floor hall alone. No one would say why, because we felt dumb. Too many spook books, we say. ...if you walked the second floor hall, the hair would stand up on your neck. It always felt as if someone was pushing you, walking way too close. When you went down the stairs to the ground floor, you must hold on to the hand rail as something was pushing you, as if someone was walking way too close and crowding you. Over the years, persons who had rented the building have come into my restaurant and told me stories of the same feeling of pushing, and of hair on end, and cold spots."

Through the years Jackie tried to accept the spirit or spirits which inhabit her space, though at times it is unnerving. Perhaps the first truly "weird" experience happened to Jackie when she was walking her three-year-old granddaughter down the hall to her upstairs apartment. The child was walking along happily until she came to a sudden stop and looked back the hall. Jackie tried to get the little girl moving again but the child kept staring down the hall as if she saw something that frightened her. Jackie looked down the hall but saw nothing.

"Come on, honey," Jackie called, trying to get the little girl moving again.

"Pick me up, Grandma! Pick me up!" Her grandchild began clinging to her. "Pick me up, please!"

"Honey, you're too heavy, now come on." Jackie gave the child's hand a little tug.

"Grandma, pick me up, please!" The child begged.

There was a tone of fear in the child's voice which galvanized Jackie. She swung the small child into her arms and hurried to the apartment.

"What did you see?", Jackie asked but her little grandchild either could not or would not tell her. This incident caused Jackie some concern. She did not want to frighten her granddaughter and she could not help wondering if the child had truly seen something that she could not see.

Late in 1989 Jackie's sister visited her and she brought along her pet dogs. From the moment her sister first entered the building, it seemed that she noticed something that Jackie had also sensed. Her sister's dogs literally refused to enter the building and never have to this day. Whatever was inside the building seemed to frighten them a great deal.

Jackie's sister had come to help Jackie work on restoring the building and one day she seemed excited or unnerved when she came to Jackie. Her sister said that she had seen a woman in a white lace blouse and long dark skirt in the second floor hallway. The woman had dark hair pinned in a bun and was pretty but very sad looking. The woman looked very solid and real, in fact her sister had wondered who the woman was and how she had gotten into the building. As Jackie's sister watched her, the woman went into a room on the second floor. Jackie's sister was close behind her. In the room the strange woman turned and stared back at Jackie's sister as she slowly faded away.

Right after Jackie opened the inn a woman came in and introduced herself. She said that she was moving to the area and was going to rent a store across the street from the Van Buren Inn. She seemed nice and Jackie welcomed her to the neighborhood. A new business on the street was good for all of the other businesses.

This woman seemed interested in the unusual architecture of the building and told Jackie that her daughter would love to tour the inn. She asked if Jackie would be in on Sunday but Jackie informed her she had plans. The women chatted a few more minutes, then the stranger left.

About a week later the woman returned, but this time she seemed upset. She sat down and told Jackie a strange story. The woman said that she had come back to Van Buren on Sunday to check out the building she wanted to rent for her flower shop. She had brought her thirteen year old daughter with her and the girl had instantly fallen in love with the inn.

The woman said that she and her daughter had peeked into the windows of the inn to get a glimpse of the building because she knew Jackie wasn't home. As they walked down the street looking into other stores, the girl lagged behind and turned back to the inn.

The thirteen year old turned to her mother. "I thought you said Jackie wouldn't be here?" she asked.

"She's not," the woman insisted. "She said she would be away today."

The girl gave her mother a quizzical look. "Yes she is. There's somebody in that second floor window."

"No, Jackie's not there!" the woman insisted.

"Mom, turn around and look. There's a woman in that window." The girl pointed toward the second floor window of the Green Room.

When the woman looked, she saw nothing, but her daughter insisted that a woman had been looking out at them.

That night the girl had a strange and frightening experience. As the thirteen year old lay in her bed, she heard voices telling her things about the inn. They told her where certain papers were hidden. Each night when the child tried to sleep, the voices returned to tell her more about the building. One voice was very upset and insistent that there were many papers about the inn building which had been taken away and were being kept in a "white house" somewhere else in town. The voices also told the girl about the unhappy woman who cries so much.

The mother was a fundamentalist Christian and this experience was unnerving and frightening to her and her daughter. She relayed what the voices said but she was clearly uncomfortable in the building.

Jackie did not tear into the walls or flooring to see if the messages were correct, but the message about the paperwork struck a note with Jackie. The person Jackie had purchased the building from had owned it for about twenty-five years. This man had told her that he had donated about two truck loads of papers from the inn to the local historical society but that the papers were being stored in an old white house a couple blocks away. How could a thirteen year old girl know about that years later?

In 1990 an older woman named Gladys, who owned an antique store across the street, came in to the restaurant one morning and seemed really rattled. The old woman asked for a cup of coffee and lit a cigarette. Jackie and Gladys always had gotten along well and she was concerned about what could have made the little, older woman so upset.

"Are you okay?" Jackie asked as she poured the coffee.

"I just saw a woman upstairs, Jackie" Gladys fidgeted nervously.

The very idea was ridiculous to Jackie. She knew that there was no one upstairs. Furthermore, she had not completed her renovations, so the second floor housed only ladders, tarps, remodeling supplies and lumber.

To Jackie it seemed best to play Gladys's statement off as a joke. "You just saw a tarp over a ladder or a shadow or lumber or something," she laughed. "There's no one up there right now."

The older woman pinned Jackie with an angry look. "I know what I saw, Jackie, and it was a woman. I pulled up to the stop sign right out front on my way to the shop. I glanced up at the building and there was a woman looking out of the second floor window. She was fairly young and pretty. She had dark hair pulled back in a bun. She wore a high-necked white blouse with lace on it and a long, dark skirt. She was just staring out the window and as I watched she slowly faded away!"

Jackie was nonplused. How could she argue with Gladys when she had experienced so many disquieting feelings herself on the second floor? The older woman was really rattled and sat drinking coffee for quite a while. Jackie tried not to upset her more by asking further questions, but it was hard.

Weeks later Jackie was baby-sitting her granddaughter one evening while her daughter was working. Jackie and her male companion were laying on their bed reading; her granddaughter was laying between them. At the foot of the bed were Jackie's two pet dogs. It was about ten p.m. when Jackie and her friend heard a sound from the stairwell. At the same time the two dogs jumped off the bed and ran to the door. The dogs were agitated, were barking and growling at the door. Jackie and her friend heard the sound of a woman walking up the stairs crying.

Jackie waited for her daughter's customary knock. She turned to her friend and sighed. "She must have had a fight with her boyfriend," she said.

For long minutes Jackie waited for the knock while dreading the thought of hearing her daughter's upsetting story. At length, she finally slipped off the bed and padded to the door to look out. Was her daughter just sitting on the steps crying?

Jackie turned the door knob and the dogs bolted past her. They made not a sound as they stood on the landing looking down the dark stairwell. They just stood there as if watching someone intently, but Jackie could see no one. She felt unnerved because the sound of a woman crying had been so real and so had the foot steps. No one could have turned and gone back down the stairs without making any noise.

Jackie turned and called her friend. She told him that she thought someone might have broken in. Her male friend retrieved Jackie's gun and together they begin searching the building for the intruder, but they found no one and no source of entry either. An hour later Jackie's daughter did come to pick up her child.

Jackie had always felt uncomfortable opening her apartment door. For many years when she went to the door and pulled it open, she had the strangest sense that someone was just on the other side. As she walked through the doorway, it always felt like some one else was there invading her body space. In the beginning, Jackie actually had to force herself to open the door, but recently that uncomfortable feeling had faded away.

Guests who stay at the bed and breakfast have occasionally complained of hearing someone taking a bath in the middle of the night even when there were no other guests. They complain that the hot water heater has been turned off, but Jackie never turns it off. Other guests have heard foot steps, and heard doors open on their own.

One day three people walked into the inn and spoke to Jackie. The group was comprised of a mother, adult daughter and a man whom the mother had recently begun seeing. The group was interested in the inn and asked to look around. The man returned to the Green Room where Jackie was and told her that she had ghosts at the inn. He said that he saw a couple he referred to as "the bank president and his wife." The man pointed to an area and asked Jackie if she could see the bank president and his wife? Jackie saw nothing and quizzed him. The man told her that the couple were very confused because their home was constantly changing, but that they seemed to be comforted by the fact that Jackie had stayed so long and was taking care of their home now.

One night a young couple knocked on Jackie's door and asked if they could spend the night. They had a four month old baby with them but Jackie welcomed them despite her policy of no children. She figured that the little baby could cause no damage, and as she had no other guests at the time, the infant's crying would cause no complaints. Jackie was tired so she showed the couple to their room and made sure they were settled before she excused herself and went to bed. She literally spent only moments talking to the young couple and she never mentioned ghosts to them.

In the morning the young woman came downstairs and asked Jackie if she had used the bathroom next to their room to take a bath in the middle of the night.

"No," Jackie said. She had her own bathroom in her apartment. "Why?"

The young woman seemed to be growing upset. Around three a.m. someone had turned on the water in the bathroom and filled the tub. There was no mistaking the sound of water hitting the bottom of the tin tub. The young woman had gotten up to check the baby when she heard it and had thought it odd for Jackie to be taking a bath at that hour.

"Well it wasn't me. Honey, I don't know what to tell ya," Jackie said. "If your husband was next to you and the baby is too little, then I don't know what to tell ya."

The young woman blanched visibly and left the restaurant. Her husband told Jackie that his wife was upset. The young man seemed embarrassed about the incident, but his wife was definitely upset by the realization that she had heard a ghost.

One evening Jackie got ready for a date after cleaning the bed and breakfast until about six-thirty. Jackie decided that she'd mop her way out of the building as she left to go on her date. It had rained hard that evening, but by the time her date brought her back, around midnight, the rain had ended.

Jackie let herself inside the building and started upstairs. She turned the lights on as she went and wasn't really thinking about anything in particular when something caught her eye and she suddenly stopped at the top of the second floor. There were big muddy footprints on the carpeting. At first Jackie thought, "How did I do that? I didn't know my feet were dirty." She placed her one foot over the print and froze. The print was larger than her shoe and shaped very differently, it was a pointy-toed print like a man in cowboy boots might make.

Now Jackie was frightened. Had someone broken in while she was gone? Was the man still there? She hurriedly let herself into the apartment and ran to the phone. Quickly she called her boyfriend and told him about the muddy prints and her fear that someone had broken in. "...I'm gonna search the building with my gun. If you don't hear from me in about five minutes, call the police," Jackie said before hanging up.

Jackie got her gun and began checking out the building, but a couple minutes later three police cars and her boyfriend pulled up outside. As she let them in, her boyfriend told her he had feared for her safety and had called the police immediately.

Jackie apprised the police of the situation and took them upstairs to see the muddy prints. The officers began a thorough search of the building while Jackie waited in the second floor hall with her boyfriend. When the police found nothing, they returned to Jackie.

The officers examined the prints again. One of the officers stood up and looked at Jackie.

"Jackie, do you notice anything odd?" he asked.

"No, what do you mean?" Jackie looked at the prints again.

"Look down those stairs," the officer indicated the steps Jackie had come up after her date. Jackie looked at them and suddenly she understood what he meant. There was no mud on the stairs. The footsteps started about six or seven feet down one side of the landing, crossed the little landing and went up the step to the other side and faded into the Green Room. Automatically her eyes pivoted toward the other end of the hall where there was the only other access, and there was no mud there either. It was as if the footsteps had materialized from nowhere and faded again into nothing.

The police could do nothing about Jackie's spectral visitor, so they left her alone. Jackie was a bit shaken by the experience but she was glad that several police officers and her boyfriend had also seen the mysterious muddy prints. It made her feel validated. At least whatever was happening at the inn was something that even the police could experience.

The muddy footprints from a man were a precursor to Jackie's introduction to her male ghost. One evening Jackie was cleaning the bed and breakfast and it was growing dark. She was dusting and did not bother to turn on the lights as she knew the Green Room well. She was singing as she dusted the room. There was a table with a mirror on the wall behind it. Jackie dusted the table and as she rose up from her work she glanced into the mirror to see a man standing behind her. He was about thirty-five years old, clean shaven with short blond hair, good looking, a white buttoned shirt and plain black jacket. The man was just standing there with his hands at his sides, staring at her in the glass.

With a scream she whirled around. "Shit! How did he get in the building?" she wondered! She looked around but found nothing. "Okay, Jackie", she told herself. "You just saw something that *looked* like a man." Jackie went back to the mirror and tried to find anything that could reflect and give her the clear image of a man she had seen, but there was nothing. All that should have been reflected in the mirror was a large double-doored armoire.

A while after this incident Jackie had a guest named Becky at the inn whom she particularly liked. One night, after Becky had been at the inn for about a week, the two women went out for dinner. After they returned to the inn Jackie began to tell her about her sighting of the man, but Becky immediately stopped her.

"No, don't," Becky said. "You let me tell you." Becky proceeded to describe the man to an amazed Jackie.

"You know you have a picture of him," Becky said.

Jackie had no idea what she was talking about, so Becky led her up to the second floor to the Green Room where Jackie had a box of old photographs from the area that guests could look at. She had purchased the box from Gladys who owned the antique store a few years earlier. Gladys, in turn, had gotten them from an estate sale about three blocks from the inn. The family who had owned the photographs had suffered a tragedy. The daughter had slain the mother and the estate of the mother had subsequently been sold off. Gladys had gotten the photographs in a box lot.

Becky dug through the pictures and came up with the one she was after. "Here," she said, holding out the photograph. "I was looking at these earlier and this man just caught my eye. He seemed *special*; I just knew it. There was just something about the eyes."

Jackie took the photograph and looked at it closely. Staring up at her was the very same man she had seen in the mirror!

Many folks had experienced phenomena at the inn, but Jackie alone had heard anyone crying and she was the only person to see the man's spirit as well. One cold, rainy winter afternoon that would all change.

It was the type of day when people preferred to stay inside away from the cold. It was lunch time and there were about a dozen or so regular customers in the restaurant. Jackie was busy making lunches and serving when a couple she had never seen before came in. She greeted them and got them settled. The wife chatted a few seconds and told Jackie that they were from Nashville and had never been in Van Buren before. They had been traveling and had pulled off in Van Buren to eat and rest a little bit before continuing on. Jackie gave them their menus and continued her work.

She saw the couple reading the back of the menu which gave a brief history of the building and made a vague reference to the possible haunting.

When Jackie returned to take their order, the wife engaged Jackie in conversation again. She told Jackie that she was psychic and had an act she did in Nashville where she read palms and offered psychic information. She offered to read Jackie's palm and Jackie let her. The customers had thinned out and Jackie had a few minutes to spare. The woman was good and told Jackie a few interesting things, but Jackie was not overly impressed. It was all just for fun and they had a few good laughs about it.

The couple asked if they could tour the house while Jackie fixed their lunch. "Go right ahead," Jackie said and she hurried off to start their order.

The couple got up and left. About ten minutes later they returned. The woman told Jackie that she had sensed two spirits in the house. One was a gentleman from the Civil War who walked with a limp and used a cane. "You have a very, very unhappy woman up there. Do you ever hear any crying?" the psychic asked.

Jackie went cold because this woman seemed to know of her experiences.

One evening after this occurrence another couple was staying in the Green Room. It was growing dark, and the husband was seated in a chair across the room. His wife had her back to him as she made them coffee. She felt a breeze behind her and she had the impression that a man had just walked past her. She turned toward the movement expecting her husband, but no one was there. She glanced back and saw that her husband was still seated across the room.

"That's odd," she remarked. "I was just going to tell you to stay put and that I'd bring your coffee to you. I could have sworn that some one was behind me." As the wife turned back to finish making coffee, her eye caught the mirror in front of her and she froze. Behind her was a man of about thirty-five to thirty-eight years. He was tall, pleasant looking and had blond hair. He wore a white shirt and black jacket. He appeared to just be standing there with his arms at his sides staring at her. She whirled around, but no one was there.

The next morning the woman told Jackie of her unnerving experience and Jackie was dumfounded. The couple had checked in late on the previous day and Jackie had only spoken to them briefly. She knew they were from out of state and they told her they had never been to Van Buren before. Jackie knew she had not told them about her ghosts so this woman's experience seemed to validate her own sighting earlier.

In the mid-1990s Jackie was contacted by a local girl scout troop. Jackie ran a little theater group in the area and the scout leader wanted to know if Jackie's group would put on a play for the girl scouts. Jackie was happy to oblige.

As it was close to Halloween, the scout leader told Jackie that the girls also wanted a ghost story. Jackie decided to tell the girls about the many haunting experiences at the inn. She set various members of her theater group in the different rooms to "haunt" them. They were to move things, make curtains sway and turn on the water in the bathrooms. While her friends haunted the inn, Jackie would take the girls through and tell them the many stories about the place.

In order to lend an air of darkness which would unnerve the girls and allow the "haunters" to move around without being detected, Jackie loosened the bulbs in the chandeliers on the second floor so they would appear not to work. Jackie would then take the girls around by lamp light.

The night of the tour and the play arrived and about 125 girls between the age of 13 and 18 came along with some parents and scout leaders. Jackie decided to take the girls around in small groups of about ten so she had to make twelve tours while she told her stories. Jackie had candles lit throughout the building and lamps burned everywhere giving the inn a very eerie touch. The girls were thoroughly frightened and everyone had a wonderful time.

The next day was a Sunday and Jackie set about straightening up the inn. She took a ladder up to the second floor so that she could screw back in all of the light bulbs on the chandeliers which she had loosened for the tours.

As Jackie worked a terrible smell suddenly enveloped her, making her almost gag. At first it smelled like rotting vegetation or something rotting. It was a terrible, choking smell. Jackie had leased out the restaurant to a local woman for a year and her first response to the terrible smell was, "What are they cooking down there?" But suddenly it struck her that it was Sunday and the restaurant was not open on Sunday. No one was cooking anything downstairs.

Jackie finished tightening the bulbs quickly and got down. She looked for a source for the smell. It was localized around the ladder area and by now she thought that the smell was more like a dead mouse. "Great," she thought the guests will be greeted by that smell for a few days. Really great for business!"

Jackie moved the ladder to the next chandelier in the hallway while thinking that at least she would not have to contend with that stench while she re-screwed these bulbs. Jackie climbed the ladder and began turning in the bulbs. Suddenly she was overwhelmed by that terrible stench again. This time the smell was worse and even stronger than before. It was literally gagging her now.

Jackie climbed down the ladder once more and again tried to locate the smell. It was again localized around the ladder. Jackie began making jokes to calm herself. "Jeez, Jackie," she said aloud. "You need to shower more or use a different deodorant or something!" She tried to laugh at her small joke but it wasn't funny.

Jackie moved the ladder into the Green Room and climbed up to tighten the bulbs in the chandelier in the room. Suddenly the stench overwhelmed her again. This time, though, it was accompanied by the most intense sensation of fear she had ever felt. Her skin literally rippled with fear and it was almost mindless. Jackie got down and hurried downstairs. She paused only long enough to get her keys before rushing outside. Never in all of her years at the inn had she ever felt anything as powerful and frightening as that intense fear she had just experienced.

It took Jackie a day and a half to even work up her courage enough to consider returning to the house. She called several people and explained what had happened. She needed to know what she had to do to banish whatever was in the inn in order for her to be able to get back into her house. Eventually Jackie managed to return home and banished the terrible entity. Jackie became convinced that her Halloween haunting night had caused the entity to enter her home.

"I have since then made a vow that ouija boards are not allowed, seances are not allowed, psychics are not allowed. I don't have any spooky movies in my house, no books. I try to avoid anything that will give it any channel or avenue because I feel that what I did by doing the tour was to give whatever it was energy. The only thing that was so different was that because this did make me feel sheer terror and the smell--it was almost as if something was just right there. It was a whole different thing than I felt all these years in this building. I've never ever been that frightened. I've been frightened of my own shadow, by hearing footsteps right behind me, things like this, but I um... This was totally different. By whatever we did we gave energy I feel to something, so I don't allow any of that kind of thing in my building because I have to live here!"

Whatever Jackie did to banish *something* frightening she believed had been called in by her Halloween tour, did not also banish the ghosts at the inn. In 1998 five women came to stay at the inn. In the morning one of the ladies casually mentioned to Jackie that a spirit had visited them during the night. She said she had been reading and the other ladies were sleeping when she felt somebody walking across the floor. She felt that the entity stood by her bed before it turned and she heard the spirit walk away.

Through the years Jackie has learned a great deal about the building she now lives in. The only violence attached to the building seems to have occurred on the third floor in the 1930's. During that time the third floor was used as a speakeasy. A local fellow began to suspect that his wife was cheating on him with another fellow. He found out that they often met at the speakeasy. The jilted husband borrowed a shotgun and sat on the second floor landing of the building smoking cigarettes and waiting for his wife's lover to come. At length the lover arrived and the jilted husband stood up, raised the gun and shot the fellow when he reached the second floor landing. The lover fell backward and rolled down the steps. He fell out the open door at the bottom and lay bleeding on the sidewalk beside the building. Local witnesses said he died right before the inn as he lay on the pavement.

There have been no bank robberies that she ever learned of and she had found no connection to the Civil War which would explain the man with a limp and cane. Yet there very well could have been a connection which has been lost in the mists of time. She is not sure who the woman is, but she might be the wife of one of the bank presidents. There are many questions left which Jackie can not answer, but she is sure of one thing; Jackie believes that those spirits haunting the Van Buren are harmless. They seem sad and lonely and perhaps should be pitied more than feared. However if you want to experience an active haunting spend some time at the Van Buren Inn. This building's spirits are very active indeed.

> *The Van Buren Inn can be contacted by writing Old Van Buren Inn and Bed & Breakfast, 633 Main Street, Van Buren Arkansas 72957 or by phoning (501) 474-4202. You can contact the department of tourism for the city of Van Buren by phoning 1-800-332-5889 or on the web at http://www.vanburen.org.*

SHARON TATE'S GHOSTLY WARNING

Darkly handsome, twenty-nine year old Jay Sebring was a young man on the move. He could not believe his own good fortune but he knew that he would continue to work hard to keep it. Jay was a man's hair stylist to the stars. His client list included actors Paul Newman, George Peppard, Frank Sinatra, Peter Lawford and many others. He was beginning to achieve success in his profession, and he was engaged to one of the most beautiful women in the world. Sharon Tate, his fiancee, was a leggy, buxom, blond with style, brains and talent. She was a young woman on her way up in the film industry. Jay was looking forward to a future as Sharon's husband when he had first decided to buy the house.

There had been something magical about the Bavarian-style house at 9860 Easton Drive, Benedict Canyon, Los Angeles, California which had seemed to reach out to Jay's sense of whimsy. The house was set back in the shade of the trees and looked for all the world like it belonged to another time, and perhaps it did. There was an old-world charm about the place which was offset by one of his favorite features. The gutter spouts on the house were hand-carved, wooden effigies of the past's most famous movie stars. Mary Pickford and Rudolph Vanentineo were among the elite carved in wood at the house. The house had style and image-conscious Sebring admired that.

The house had once been owned by Hollywood's original blond beauty, Jean Harlow and her much older husband, MGM producer Paul Bern in the 1930's.

Harlow and Bern had lived a tumultuous life in the house. Bern had beaten Harlow severely several times. It was later said that Harlow had died of kidney failure because of a beating she had received from Bern. Their friends and acquaintances said that Bern had a bad temper and was extremely jealous of his twenty-one year old sex symbol wife. He both adored the fact that other men desired Jean and despised her for it.

Jean Harlow seemed to adore her husband publicly and despite the beatings she stayed with him. Years later some people acquainted with Harlow would say that Jean had been having an affair with another man and that Bern knew about it. Bern, it seemed, was a dud in the bedroom because he was endowed with an extremely small penis and Harlow taunted him about that. She flaunted her lovers and drove Bern crazy, or so friends would later say. Ultimately, only Bern and Harlow knew the true state of their relationship, but friends and business partners would later put forth several theories as to why Jean stayed with Bern and why Bern abused Jean.

Whatever the state of their relationship was, the two lived and died in the house in Benedict Canyon which Jay Sebring now owned. He knew that Paul Bern had committed suicide in the master bedroom of the house by shooting himself, and that a couple years later Jean Harlow had succumbed to kidney failure.

There were stories that two people had drowned in the pool there after Harlow's death. It seemed that the house had seen its share of sorrow.

There was the usual Hollywood gossip about the house being haunted and that those who lived there seemed to become jinxed, but Sebring wasn't worried. He enjoyed the stories about the house and thought they added excitement and charm to the place. In fact, he told friends that one of the reasons he bought the house was its "far out" reputation.

The house was charming and Sharon Tate must have thought it was lovely at first, but one night that all changed. Later she would recount that night's events to several people, including a reporter named Dick Kleiner who interviewed her.

On this night in 1966 Sharon was alone in the house. Jay had gone to Europe on business and had asked her to house-sit for him. Sharon had agreed, but now she found herself feeling very "odd" and uncomfortable. Every little sound made Sharon jumpy and nervous. At last Sharon decided that she could stand no more and went up to bed.

In the master bedroom she crawled between the sheets and tried to fall asleep, but sleep seemed far away. Sharon had left the bedroom lights on to help her ward off her nervousness but the light did little to dispel her queer feelings.

As she lay in bed wide awake and trying to convince herself that she had nothing to fear, the bedroom door was suddenly opened by a small man with a clipped mustache and dark, thinning hair. The man gave her the creeps and she knew immediately that this was Paul Bern--or at least what was left of him.

In a panic Sharon watched as Bern began moving around the bedroom. He concentrated upon the desk area as he searched for something. He muttered to himself as he searched, and she slipped out of bed quickly. Tossing her robe on, Sharon darted out of the room where Bern was noisily continuing his search.

Sharon darted for the stairs and began to run down them. Suddenly she froze in horror. Below her on the steps was the most horrifying scene she had ever witnessed. It was a figure of a person, but she could not tell for sure if it was male or female. The person had been lashed to the stairs newel post by a rope and the figure's throat was slit.

Sharon stared at the terrible tableau for precious seconds as her mind struggled to comprehend what her eyes saw. Behind her she could hear Bern's ghost and before her lay death bound to the stair posts. At last Sharon bolted past the apparition on the stairs and ran into the living room. To steady her nerves she thought she'd have a drink but she could not find where Jay had put his liquor.

Suddenly, she would later tell Kleiner, she had a strong impression that she should push on one of the bookcases. Sharon threw her weight against the shelves and they gave way, revealing a fully stocked bar. Sharon poured herself a drink.

Shaking and terrified Sharon forced herself to try and be calm and reasonable. She had to get hold of herself and be rational about what had happened, but that was going to be hard. As she sat there trying to convince herself to be calm, an overwhelming impulse seemed to overcome her and she bolted toward the bar again. She found herself frantically tearing at the base of the bar; pulling away the wallpaper there. Her efforts were rewarded and she found that she had revealed a solid copper bar base.

Amazingly, Sharon suddenly felt herself calming down and she began to feel as if she were in a dream. She left the living room, walked past the blood soaked figure still lashed to the banister posts and started up the stairs. She could see and hear Bern's specter who was now in the hallway before her, but suddenly she was not so afraid. She entered the master bedroom, took off her robe and laid down. Almost immediately Sharon was asleep.

In the morning Sharon awoke a bit worse for the alcohol and feeling groggy. She remembered her terror-filled night, but thought that the whole thing had been a nightmare. Sharon tried to shake off the terrible feelings the dream had left her with, and she started downstairs. In the living room she froze. One of the book cases was opened to reveal a stocked bar and there was wallpaper strewn about the floor below the bar area.

Where the wallpaper had been ripped away, she could clearly see a solid brass bar base. The night's events came crashing back once more. If the dream of finding the secret bar and tearing away the wallpaper had not been a dream, did that mean that all of the past night's events *had* happened?

Sharon did not know it but about three years later she would find herself bound and tied up in another house only a few miles from this one. She would be mutilated and covered in blood, and so would the house's new owner, Jay Sebring. Jay would be tied to the other end of the rope that bound Sharon and would be shot trying to protect his former fiancee, and now good friend who had left him to marry another man. He would die trying to save nine-month pregnant Sharon Tate Polanski and her baby from death at the hands of the crazed Manson Family murderers.

Perhaps the house was cursed by the evil that had taken Paul Bern, Jean Harlow and the two swimmers, or could it be that the house or the spirits in it were trying to give Sharon Tate a warning glimpse of her own future? Had they tried to warn her that she and Jay were going to die nearby, at 10050 Cielo Drive, while bound by ropes?

THE SPIRITS OF QUARANTINE STATION, AUSTRALIA

So much has changed during the twentieth century that we find it difficult to believe that there was a time in the history of the world when strangers traveling were considered a hazard to the countries they wanted to enter. People barely remember why places like Ellis Island in the United States and Quarantine Station near Sydney, Australia ever existed but they served a vital function. Many countries had places where people could be screened so that disease did not enter and ravage the land. Sicknesses we now take as common such as the flu could wipe out hundreds of thousands of people, so the authorities were justified in their concerns. Today we simply board a plane and in a matter of hours we're at our destination, but it was far different in the past. Ship voyages could last weeks or even months and hygiene aboard ship was spotty at best. This was a breeding ground for disease and many who arrived on foreign shores did so with an illness that needed treated.

In Australia Spanish influenza, cholera, bubonic plague and tuberculosis had taken a terrible toll. In the port city of Sydney there was a very real fear that a ship could come into the harbor which would carry a deadly disease. People fleeing oppression and poverty sought refuge in Australia's vast climes, but they often brought with them illnesses that were impossible for the doctors of that day to fight. That was why the Australian authorities passed a law called the Quarantine Act which was passed in 1832 to establish a quarantine center where immigrants could be screened and treated. This act of reason would protect the people of Australia for more than 100 years before the center was closed.

The spot chosen for the Quarantine Station was North Head Island. This bit of land seemed tailored for just such a proposition. It had an area which would make a good harbor, it was isolated from the mainland of Australia so that contagions could be contained and it had enough room so that the facilities, including graveyards, could expand as needed. The Quarantine Station was built and at one time took up much more than its present 69 acres.

At its zenith, the station was accepting up to eight ships full of immigrants per day. During this time they often ran out of housing for the many people and the healthy folks were forced to seek make-shift accommodations upon the beaches and hills of the island. Those who were sick were cared for in the hospital, but those who were well were often pressed into service to help build new buildings, dig graves or do other chores. With nothing else to do, many people were glad to have the distraction of work.

People often spent several months at Quarantine Station and the stories of sickness and disease they told were terrible. There was a sense of desperation and hopelessness that permeated the island. People hoping for a better life were discouraged and often died with their hopes shattered. The people who worked there tried to save as many folks as they could, but still the death toll was staggering. One ship captain named Stokes wrote that he recognized Quarantine Station by the number of headstones on the hillsides. The dead and dying were never ending in those days.

The doctors and nurses who staffed the Station were a brave lot, but like those who served in the medical units in wartime, they were casualties of their own desires to help.

Some of the staff contracted diseases and perished, others could not escape the memories so it is not surprising that stories of the hauntings of Quarantine Station are legion.

The station was shut down as a quarantine station before World War One, but was reactivated so that returning veterans could be isolated there until their health could be verified. They had been exposed to the influenza which swept the world beginning in 1918 and the Australians vainly tried to stop the spread of this decease to their shores. Worldwide this plague killed millions. The buildings were shut down and not used again until they were needed to house the refugees from Vietnam who sought asylum upon Australian shores. The Quarantine station also was reopened to house the victims of Cyclone Tracy which devastated so many.

In 1984 the buildings were handed over to the National Parks and Wildlife Service to be absorbed into the Sydney Harbor National Park System. Despite now officially being part of the Sydney National Park, Quarantine Station remains aloof, a city which stands alone. It has its own morgue, hospital, water and power supply, post office, and telephone system. There are paved streets with lovely homes and a scenic view of the ocean and the beach below it to recommend it.

Today the National Parks and Wildlife Service keeps the center open as a tourist attraction and the main attraction are the spirits. Each evening there are three hour tours of the Station and it's sixty buildings. Each tourist is given a lantern as they prepare to walk the ground where so many before them had come in hope and so many never left.

The tour winds through the hospital, the morgue and the various other buildings including the barracks where the refugees and migrants were housed. A tour guide tells stories about the many people said to haunt the station and about the many folks who have experienced the hauntings.

In the hospital many people have described phantom doctors and nurses who hurry by on missions never completed. When these phantom care givers are approached or spoken to, they vanish. Other people have complained about feeling a deep depression or experiencing cold spots in the hospital area.

By far the most commonly reported ghosts in the hospital wards, though, are the ghosts of patients. People have long told tales of seeing people in beds in the two hospital wards only to turn away and look back and find the patients gone. Most folks report that the ghosts of Quarantine Station are transparent though very real looking.

In the Australian Ghost Hunting Association (AGHA) website they report a story about a tourist who pointed out that one of the bath tubs was dirty. He joked that he could see names written in the grime and insinuated that the matron who supposedly haunted the area had better start doing a better job of cleaning. As soon as he uttered the words, the man grew violently ill. He had to rush outside to throw-up. The sudden sickness refused to abate and for a long while the poor man repeatedly grew violently ill. At last he seemed to recover slightly, though the guide who tended to him reported that the man was very pale and shaken. Still the man wanted to finish the tour so he went on.

As he walked up the hills, he heard heavy breathing behind him as if someone was having a hard time climbing. The man commented upon the steep climb to this person, but received no response. Upon turning, he realized that there was no one there. The other people in the group were at least fifteen feet away from him and none of them seemed to be suffering from labored breathing. This finally terrified the man and he turned back down the hill. The man broke into a run and a tour guide followed to attend him once more. After the guide caught up to the badly frightened man the guide tried vainly to comfort him. The ghosts at Quarantine Station had never been violent and were always benign. The man was unimpressed. He informed the guide that he had agreed to the tour but had been a total skeptic, now he was a confirmed believer in spirits.

During this same tour there were other unusual incidents reported the AGHS. A tour guide walking through the linen closet area heard a distinct pounding upon the closet door. It was odd for the door to be closed and even odder that someone had been shut in there. The guide suspected that someone was trying to scare them so the guide pulled open the door. No one was in the closet despite the fact that the guide and the entire group had heard the thumping of someone trying to get out.

An unusual feature of Quarantine Station is the fact that you can sleep over in the newer brick section of the hospital which is known as the second ward. Before the public was allowed to sleep in the building the staff felt they should test out the idea. They were not worried about spirits, but were concerned about the comfort level for their guests. Nine guides volunteered to sleep in the second ward. One of the female guides had an experience that night that she will never forget. Before dawn she was frightened awake by hands that were forcing her into a sitting up position. Terrified, the woman tried not to look at what held her up but she could not help seeing a white mass close beside her. She tried to scream for help from the other guides but she could not make a sound. Silently she mouthed the words "go away" repeatedly and the apparition finally let her go.

During the sleep-overs several people have reported hearing carts being pushed around or feeling someone touching them during the night. The phenomena is reported most often by people sleeping in the same bed the female guide had slept in.

The Mortuary is probably one of the most haunted areas. People talk about the heavy atmosphere which could be imagination, but many of the other events certainly are not. In the 1920's and 1930's two ladies lived in the Station and they often spoke of the spirits they encountered. One of the spirits was a sailor who looked forever out of the one window at the mortuary.

There is a window in the Mortuary which has an unusual story attached to it. According to the story an aboriginal man from the shops grew ill and died in the Station. His body was taken to the mortuary where it was laid out. During that night a terrible lightning storm blew up and lightning crashed all around the area. In the morning employees entered the morgue and were shocked to see the aboriginal's likeness etched in the glass. Some people claim to clearly see this image while others can't see anything remotely like a face.

The tour guides tell another story which is much more alarming. A lady taking the tour one night appeared upset and frightened upon leaving the morgue. Her story was indeed terrifying. She claimed that the entire time the tour guide was explaining about the mortuary she had seen a man's body laying upon one of the slabs. The man opened his eyes and fixed them upon her. "Look what they've done to me! Look what they've done to me," he moaned as he threw back the sheet to expose his mutilated body. He was showing her the autopsy incision which ran the length of his torso. The woman looked at this apparition in horror and couldn't understand why no one else was reacting. Apparently she alone could see and hear this man. The staff assured her that no one was playing tricks and the other tourists in her group agreed that they neither saw nor heard anything.

People have had doors slam in their faces, and the sound of slamming doors comes from the mortuary when no one is there.

Perhaps the most disturbing part of the Quarantine Station tour begins when visitors are ushered into the shower block. If there is any malignant energy left from this institution's past, it is here. Psychics and sensitive people have repeatedly confirmed a terrible presence in the corners of the showers. Interestingly enough, psychics have all told the same story after visiting this area. They feel that a terrible sexual assault upon a small child happened in one corner of the area. Tourists often comment upon feeling an "evil presence" in that same corner and still others have come away badly shaken after hearing the unearthly cries of the tortured child.

Perhaps the presence there simply likes to unnerve people, or perhaps there are more spirits haunting the shower block for the rest of the haunting is more benign. It is a common occurrence for the lights to switch themselves on and off in this area. Light bulbs often explode and a tremendous banging, as if someone is striking heavy tin, occurs quite often.

A story is told of a local fellow who took his family on a tour of Quarantine Station. The man tried to hurry them through the showers area because of its reputation and because there was at that time no electrical power hooked up in the building and it was growing dark. His family insisted upon seeing the entire station, shower block included, and the man felt constrained to oblige. Upon entering the shower area this fellow noticed an electrical outlet box with exposed wires dangling out. To be sure that there was no power because those exposed wires could be dangerous, the man flipped the light switches several times. Nothing happened.

As they toured the building in the growing twilight, they reached the third shower area which is the end of the showers. The man knew that the door was rusted fast in the open position. Suddenly the family was jolted by the door wrenching free of it's rusted hinges and slamming shut. Immediately the lights blazed on and they heard footsteps at the far end of the shower area. In unison the family bolted from the building but they did note that as they exited the lights turned themselves back off. After a few minutes of regrouping--and I would imagine checking pulses--the more intrepid family members decided to re-enter the building to search for an explanation. When they did enter, the lights turned themselves back on once they approached the third shower area.

Another tale told by the staff is about a group of ladies having a "hen's night." The women were primed for the tour by hearing the many tales of the hauntings. They managed to make it through most of the tour without incident, but in the shower block everything changed.

As they toured that area, a shower in the third block suddenly turned itself on. The women ran out screaming. Two ladies did return to turn off the shower and they were subjected to loud banging which sent them from the building once more.

The many spirits at the Quarantine Station seem to invade every corner of the many acres. People speak of the spirit of a little girl with long braids who seeks human companionship. She has often joined tour groups and she pulls upon sleeves or hands trying to get attention. A psychic who said she had not known the stories of Quarantine Station before touring it reported seeing a girl passing through her tour group. The child paused before each woman and studied her face as if searching for someone--a lost mother perhaps?

An employee was so moved by his experience with the little girl that he wrote down his encounter. He said that one evening around sunset he went out to get in his car and go home. As he sat in the car a face suddenly appeared before him upon the windshield. He was terribly frightened and tried to find a rational explanation for it but there was none. A spirit from the station had followed him.

Down on the beach there are the wharves where so many immigrants had left their ships to come to the Station. Today people sometimes report hearing the sounds of a busy wharf and the chatter of people moving and speaking there. In an unusual note, the wharf seems fire-prone and has been damaged three times by flames. A man who worked as a caretaker at the Station often reported that the lights in his office would turn on and off by themselves. He felt distinctly uncomfortable there and asked others to accompany him if he could. He said that he felt that someone was after him in his office. The Park Service had the lights rewired in that office fearing a short which could destroy the building. The lights continued to go on and off at will despite new wiring.

Tour groups have seen white masses which follow them around or which disappear upon investigation. Some groups have seen and heard many other things including a buzzing noise which seemed to make the air "heavy" and oppressive. After one of these nights of buzzing two guides reported that their cars did not work when they tried to leave.

Others have claimed to see a Chinaman in the building. This man is in traditional dress and has a long pigtail down his back. He is obviously the spirit of a weary traveler who never made it to his destination. His grave is undoubtedly among those upon the hillsides around the Station.

Locked doors unlock themselves, doors jam and yet can be opened easily by someone else mere seconds later, lights burn in buildings where there is no electrical connection today, spirits and white ghosts float about, medicine and laundry carts are heard though no one pushes them today, ghostly faces peering out windows, phantom nurses making appointed rounds, foot steps and heavy breathing which follows visitors and staff alike are reported. White vapor mists which follow visitors and staff along the roads home have become more common. The list goes on and on. No wonder Quarantine Station is considered Australia's most haunted site. It is a good bet that anyone who wants to encounter spirits would do well to make a visit to this place. And even if the spirits don't attend your visit, you will still enjoy a wonderful tour of an unique piece of Australian history.

For more information ask your tourist Agency or you can contact Quarantine Station at North Head Scenic Drive, Manly, New South Wales, Australia, 2095 or phone them at (02) 9977-6522. Tours are very popular so be sure to plan well in advance and you must have a scheduled tour or you can not visit the site. No refunds under any circumstance.

THE GHOSTLY KITTEN

As anyone who is the parent of more than one child knows, all children are not the same. Some are very outgoing and easy to be with, but others are quiet or even painfully shy and these children need more attention than the others. That was how the Laret family felt about their little son, Rene. Despite being one of several children, Rene was different. Even the school saw this sensitive intelligence when Rene started school. He was a child who could have a brilliant future, but only if he was handled with care.

Rene was the youngest child and his parents watched over him very carefully. To draw him out of himself they gave him a little white kitten when he was seven. Rene called the kitten Jacques and the kitten quickly became his constant companion. When Rene returned home from school, his first act was to find Jacques. The kitten slept with him and seemed to be as devoted to Rene as Rene was to the kitten.

The Larets all enjoyed the kitten and were glad that it gave Rene an outlet for the immense love that was locked inside his little heart. They allowed him to take the kitten with him a few places and they all watched out for the kitten lest something happen to it. But one Saturday morning in the summer of 1954 Jacques got out and was struck down by a truck.

The Larets were horrified to find the poor little white kitten dead and their first thought was how would Rene handle the loss? Rene, however, did not seem to miss the kitten that first day. He never seemed to be looking for the kitten. He simply went about his Saturday as if all was fine.

By Sunday the Larets were very concerned. Why hadn't Rene asked about Jacques? Did he know somehow and was he ignoring the truth?

Mrs. Laret decided that it was necessary to make Rene face the truth. The couple sat the child down and gently told him the truth. Rene's reaction, however, was one they least expected.

Rene jumped up and with tears streaming from his eyes, he screamed that they were wrong. "Jacques is alive! He is alive!" the boy wailed. "He is here with me. Can't you see him?"

The conviction in the child's voice froze his mother. Was it possible that the child had convinced himself his little kitten was alive to avoid the pain of the loss?

From that moment on the family decided to humor Rene. Perhaps in time he would accept the truth, but until then they allowed him to pretend that the little kitten was alive. He hurried home each day to put out food and milk for the little kitten. He would sit and stroke the air and pretend that the kitten was there. He would talk to the dead kitten and insisted on carrying the little animal into his room. The sight of Rene pretending broke his parents' hearts.

After weeks of pretending Charles Laret decided to take matters into his own hands. "Rene, you know that Jacques is gone and you mustn't pretend anymore," he told his son one night. "Jacques is not coming back."

The boy looked hurt and confused. "But, papa, can't you see Jacques? He's right here at my feet sleeping," the child insisted. No amount of trying would shake Rene of his conviction that his little kitten was with him.

Weeks turned into months and the Larets were growing ever more concerned, for Rene never tired of pretending that Jacques was with him.

The couple decided to seek help for Rene and finally contacted a Dr. Lefeve who was a prominent psychiatrist. After testing the child the doctor told the couple that Rene was perfectly fine. "But how can that be, doctor," Michelle Laret demanded. "Rene sees an invisible cat!"

"You see, " the doctor explained, "Rene simply is convinced that the cat is there. He believes it is with him, so the cat is with him. He is operating under a conviction that nothing ever happened to take his cat away. He is completely sane but he is totally convinced that the cat is real, so it is real to him."

Charles Laret stared at the doctor in amazement. "Do you mean that the cat is a ghost?"

"I don't believe in ghosts," Dr. Lefeve stated. "However, we can make a few tests in your home to see what will happen."

The family agreed to the tests and the Dr. Lefeve set them up. Dr. Lefeve found out that whenever Rene entered a room with the cat the temperature dropped several degrees. However, if Rene entered alone there was no drop in temperature. Dr. Lefeve also dusted the floors, the fireplace mantle and other areas where Jacques supposedly walked. Amazingly enough, tiny cat paw prints appeared in the powder even when Dr. Lefeve was watching and controlling the situation.

Dr. Lefeve left the Larets without forming any conclusions; he and the Larets just could not believe in ghostly cats.

One day the couple dressed Rene up and told him they were going to get his picture taken. As they settled the children into the car, Rene insisted on rushing back to the house for Jacques so he could have his picture taken, too. The couple sighed but allowed Rene to carry his invisible cat in his lap.

At the photography studio they waited as Rene was posed, and here he again insisted upon settling the invisible cat into his lap so that it could appear in the photograph. By now the Larets had nearly resigned themselves to Rene's eccentricity. What harm was there in allowing an invisible cat to appear in the picture?

When the photograph of Rene was retrieved from the photography studio, the Larets were terribly shocked. Rene had been sitting with his arms across his chest and there, nestled in his arms was a small white kitten. It was most definitely Jacques!

The couple contacted Dr. Lefeve again and he was astonished to see the amazing photograph. Dr. Lefeve arranged to have the photograph and negative studied and it is not believed to have been tampered with. The only conclusion the doctor and the Laret family could come up with is that somehow Rene's belief in Jacques was so strong that he somehow recreated the kitten or else...Rene was truly seeing a ghostly kitten.

The photograph of Rene with the ghostly Jacques was given to the French Society for Psychical Research and the family continued with their life. As for Rene and Jacques, they were truly best friends who could not be separated even by death.

LEIGH MASTERS AND SAM

In Westminster, Maryland stands an old house which has long since seen it's best days. Made of pink brick and trimmed with grey paint, Lookabout was a fine estate owned by Leigh Masters who came to America in 1774 and purchased 1,443 acres which was the beginning of a tremendous estate. Masters prospered in his ventures. Masters was a gentleman farmer, a failed politician, a businessman. He would later buy 6,000 more acres to make Lookabout one of the largest estates for miles around.

Leigh Masters did not care if his neighbors in Westminster, Maryland did not like him. As far as he was concerned, they were a bunch of rabble-rousers and traitors to his home nation of England. His reasons for leaving England were private, but that did not mean that he had to enjoy living in this new country. His neighbors tried to ingratiate themselves with him, but that only made him disdain them more.

Masters certainly didn't mind taking American money, nor did he have a problem with exploiting the resources of this rich new land. Masters made his fortune by mining iron ore and refining it in large furnaces upon his estate. He made a great fortune from iron smelting, and this gave him the independence to be as arrogant as he wanted to be.

In the Westminster area the local folks had strong opinions about Leigh Masters, too. He was a stuck up prig of a man who was downright anti-social. He disliked the local folks and would call the dogs out to chase anyone who trespassed upon his estate. Masters went further, though, and dressed as a ghost to frighten off trespassers, poachers or fishermen. He would ride after trespassers and chase them to ground. What punishment awaited the transgressors was not recorded, but stories of Masters ghostly rides at night made the rounds of the Westminster area.

Through the years his feeling about his neighbors and his politics made Masters even less liked. But it was Masters cruelty toward his slaves that made him legendary. Even the other slave owners in the area were loathe to hear about how Masters mistreated his slaves.

Masters enjoyed breaking his livestock--including his slaves. He beat the beasts of his barn and made them suffer every form of depravation imaginable if they let him down in any way. Worse treatment yet was meted out to any slave who dared show that he or she thought they might be more human than beast. He did beat and whip slaves both male and female, but there was one slave who could set Leigh Masters to anger quicker than any other. That slave was a great giant of a man named Sam. Sam seemed somehow to transcend his surroundings. He wore his shackles and took his lashes from the whip, but he was not beaten down in spirit. Sam refused to be servile to any man. This infuriated his master, who vowed that he'd break that black beast if it was the last thing he ever did. Leigh Masters was determined that Sam would kneel before him begging for mercy before he was through.

Week after week, year after year, the battle between Sam and Masters continued. Sam was clearly disadvantaged, but he was winning. Leigh Masters ordered horrible beatings that would have killed a lesser man, but they did not break Sam.

Stories of Masters cruel treatment passed through the valley by word of mouth. Slaves on the block were terror stricken if they were bought by Masters. Other whites shook their heads in disgust and muttered that there should have been something they could do. But beating a slave was not a crime, so they had no recourse but to endure the stories.

Finally Masters' fury at Sam went beyond all bounds. Masters ordered Sam tied and lashed until he was satisfied. During the beating he would stop the lashes and demand of Sam that if he bowed to his master, Sam could be cut down. Sam glowered at the monster before him, but he would not bow.

Masters threatened terrible deaths if Sam did not bow, but still the enslaved man held his ground. Masters ordered more lashes but still Sam would not submit.

At last Masters seemed driven to madness by this slave's bravery. He ordered that one of the iron ore furnaces be built up to it's hottest.

Masters roared at Sam that he would roast him alive. Sam still did not cower before the beastly man who owned him. Masters dragged Sam's battered body down to the furnaces. Those around him wanted to help Sam, but they could not, lest Masters' rage turn on them, too.

Helplessly Sam was dragged to the very brink of the furnace. One last time Sam was ordered to grovel, but to Sam there were things worse than death. He held his battered head up and glared at Masters.

Masters threw Sam into the oven alive. The terrible screams from Sam rent the air, but Masters knew no pity.

It did not take long for the story of Sam's death to leave the estate. Slaves passed the story along from one plantation to another and the white masters heard the story, too. Still, what could they legally do? Killing a slave was not a crime, so they just shook their heads and determined not to do business with the monster of Masters' estate. Of course, no one could prove that Sam was roasted alive, but Sam had suddenly disappeared. That fact was not wasted upon any who knew Masters.

For the slaves that Masters owned, the disappearance of Sam seemed to begin a terrible new chapter for them. Having at last assigned one man to the ovens, Masters found this punishment most satisfactory. Stories of him cooking slaves in the ovens left the plantation in time. It was even said that he roasted children alive in order to punish the parents.

Masters became a pariah in the community, but it bothered him little. Slaves and goods could be purchased from other towns so he simply went away to do his business.

For the rest of Masters life the story of Sam's death, and stories about his many other cruelties, would follow him. When he finally died at the age of 80 the whole valley breathed a sigh of relief. Masters would no longer ride across his estate like a demonic spirit chasing any hapless soul who had the misfortune to step upon his ground. No longer would the slaves be subjected to such terrible treatment. The local folks would have been glad to see this chapter in the town's history closed, but even death did not hold down Leigh Masters.

Masters' body was interred in a tomb upon the estate but the vault was vandalized and the body had to be removed. Leigh Masters' final resting place is the Assention Episcopal Grave Yard in Westminster, Maryland.

The Bible says, "Vengeance is mine, thus sayeth the Lord," and perhaps vengeance is God's, but Sam seemed to find some in the afterlife. Soon after Leigh Masters died people began saying that they saw Masters spirit running along the fields of his estate pursued by a large, black figure that could not be clearly seen. Masters seemed terrified of this figure overtaking him and ran on through the night in silent fear. Old-timers remembered Sam and his terrible death and soon they were saying that Sam had come back to seek vengeance upon Leigh Masters for his horrible life and his even more horrible death.

Masters' ghost was seen stalking the fields and forests of his estate by night. He still sought out poachers and trespassers whom he would route. He was said to chase some of them to their own front doors.

Other folks claimed to meet a headless spirit believed to be Masters astride his favorite horse. Those who encountered the headless apparition said that Masters evil spirit was often accompanied by three black imps with glowing eyes.

In the 1940's a family living in the main house on the estate said they heard the cries of a phantom infant. They told the man who lived in the tenant house. Years later that man would remember the story of a phantom baby crying when he helped tear out an old bake oven in the kitchen of the main house. He would say that behind the oven he and the other workers found the skeleton of an infant about two months old. Was it one of the children legend said Leigh Masters baked alive? Other workers would insist that they found an adult's skull behind the oven instead.

Through the years people have forgotten about Leigh Masters and the stories of his sadistic ways are no longer talked about, but perhaps Sam has not forgotten nor forgiven Masters. Perhaps through some housing complex or along some forgotten field Sam still pursues Masters late at night. And if Sam does still seek vengeance, I hope he gets it. I hope that one dark night Sam catches Masters and the wheels of justice grind him under foot.

THE HAUNTED CRESCENT HOTEL

If there has ever been a dream come true, then the Crescent Hotel in Eureka Springs, Arkansas is that dream for many. The Crescent was considered the most grand hotel and spa in America at the turn of the twentieth century.

Built of native white granite in the English Gothic style with turrets and peeked roofs, the sprawling structure sits 2,000 feet up on an Ozark mountain top like a queen wearing her jewels. Shimmering windows and grand doors give way to an interior which was awe-inspiring. The main lobby spreads before the visitor like welcoming arms. An ornate stone fireplace with chairs set around to offer the weary traveler respite gives way to a reservation desk where the most famous and richest people of the day often registered.

This was only a glimpse of what awaited the traveler. The rooms were beautifully decorated with turn-of-the century grandure, and there was a grand dining room where three meals a day were served. The rooms boasted 14 foot ceilings, balconies, glass walls, carved marble fireplaces, and luxurious furniture.

And all of this was just the beginning. There were grand balls and tea dances in the afternoons, where folks danced to the music of an in-house orchestra. Waiters in white jackets and black pants quietly circulated among the hundreds of guests taking orders and unobtrusively granting their every whim.

There was a 100 horse stable, two bowling lanes, swimming pools, tennis courts, a golf course, hiking and walking trails, tours and a specialty of the hotel, Tally-hos. These were rides upon a large wagon that could seat 35 people. The ornate wagon was pulled by a team of up to 8 matched horses.

But no one could deny that one of the principle reasons for coming to the Crescent Hotel was the water. Lake Lucerne, then called Sanitarium Lake offered a special bathing treat. There were also the springs which provided mineral waters reputed to have great healing effects.

The Crescent Hotel was run for years by the Eureka Springs Improvement Company as an exclusive year-round hotel under the management of General Powell Clayton, but even before the Crescent was finished the first ghost was said to haunt the building.

The hotel was designed to be built with the finest materials and the finest workmen were used. Among the men brought in to shape the white granite stones which form the hotel was an Irishman named Michael. No one remembers his last name today, but that does not stop Michael.

One day Michael was working upon the roof of the four story hotel when he slipped and fell. The floors of the top two stories were not yet laid down and Michael fell all of the way to the second floor where he died. The second floor area where he tragically passed away is now said to be haunted by Michael. People report seeing a young man who vanishes before their astonished eyes. But Michael does not seem to confine himself to just the second floor. He has been seen in other areas throughout the hotel including the basement.

In one report provided by the Eureka Springs Historical Museum, a local resident named Joe Head, who often bowled in one of the two lanes provided at the Crescent Hotel in the 1950's, once met Michael. He said that he had heard the laundry workers tell stories of seeing the ghost of Michael but he hadn't paid much attention to them as he did not believe in ghosts. However, all of that changed.

The bowling lanes were located in the basement and one evening Joe left them to make his way to the men's room. Along the way he saw a young man coming toward him down the long corridor. Something about the man intrigued Joe and he watched him as they neared each other. Suddenly the young man was simply gone.

"It's kind of a strange feeling. It's hard to explain," Joe later said. He wasn't frightened but he felt a bit confused. It was a matter of convincing yourself that you just saw what you thought you saw, he told the reporter. Today the area where Michael died is a health spa.

The Crescent Hotel opened on May 20th, 1886 to great fanfare. This was the best thing that had happened to the area since before the Civil War. The war had decimated much of the south and the industry that would build up around the Crescent Hotel was much needed. The local newspaper, THE DAILY TIMES-ECHO said, "The hotel is said by those who have enjoyed its hospitalities to come nearest to the ideal home of any resort hotel in America. My authority for this is a retired physician now spending, as is his custom, every year of late, his winter months here. This gentleman has traveled extensively in this country and has visited all of the famous watering places of Europe, and says that he knows of no hotel where everything is so home-like and where there is so little of the air of a health resort as at the Crescent Hotel."

It was not an accident that the Crescent Hotel was so well planned. The architect who worked tirelessly to design the grand lady was Isaac S Taylor. Taylor paid great attention to even the slightest details of the Crescent. He was extremely fond of his creation, and perhaps that is why he haunts it to this day.

After Taylor's death people at the hotel began saying that they saw a frock coated gentleman who resembled Taylor walking the halls of the Crescent Hotel. The man is harmless and seems content to walk the halls and visit the many rooms of the hotel he created. Of course, seeing a gentleman dressed in the style of the late 19th century who simply vanishes or walks into a wall is unnerving for the mortal guests, but Mr. Taylor means no harm.

A local historian, June Westphal, passed on a little incident which a friend confided to her in the 1970's. This friend worked in the hotel as the night clerk at the front desk. Several times this friend saw a man in formal evening dress from the 1890's on the main stairs in the evening. Others saw a person dressed for a formal ball coming down the stairs, this person, too, was dressed in 1890's formal attire.

In 1902 the hotel was leased to the Frisco Railroad System which remodeled it. They put in up-to-date plumbing, and electricity along with many other innovations of the day such as telephones. This was the beginning of a five year association between the railroad and the grand Ozark lady.

The Frisco Railroad System billed the hotel as a "Health-Watering Resort" and put in railroad tracks to the area so that their guests could arrive in style. Guests could either take the traditional Tally-ho ride up to the Crescent Hotel or they could ride an electric cable car up the mountain.

From this time period there dates an unusual story which might have something to do with the Crescent Hotel. Many trains came and went every day bringing guests and taking away others from the Crescent Hotel. The railroad ensured that they could arrive easily and was a boon to the hotel. Perhaps one train had not arrived yet and had been trying to deliver its load of guests until that very day.

In mid-summer of 1911 a train was headed up to Eureka Springs when it slowed down to take on a passenger in the village of Gaskins, about two miles above the Eureka Springs depot. The engineer named Dobbins saw, as they slowed down, that there was a caboose in front of them with signal lights lit. A conductor came out of the caboose and waved a warning at them with a lantern. At about the same time Dobbins noticed flares burning and he turned to shout to his fireman, a fellow named Harrelson, that something was wrong.

Harrelson took in the situation at a glance. Together he and Dobbins grabbed the reverse lever and threw it over. The men knew that they would have to act fast. They jumped to the steps and made ready to jump off. It is not easy to stop a train and it is even harder to make a train going forward go instantly into reverse. They were both aware that they would have to jump clear of both trains before they crashed into the caboose.

As Dobbins and Harrelson waited for the right moment to jump, the train with it's caboose, the conductor waving his lantern and the flares all simply disappeared. Nothing remained of the phantom train.

The men were terribly frightened by their experience. Harrelson would refuse to return the next day for the same run. Dobbins worked that same run under protest. He let everyone who would listen know that the phantom train had been a warning. He believed that there would be a terrible accident in that spot soon. But there were no train wrecks that summer and folks forgot about poor Dobbins and Harrelson and their phantom train.

Today folks can once again take the same ride as Harrelson and Dobbins. The Eureka Springs Railroad was bought by Reat Younger and his brothers who have worked at restoring it. Reat Younger tells the story along with the history of the little railroad in his book entitled, **JUST A LITTLE TRAIN TRIP**. The railroad is located in the town of Beaver, and it might be worth a detour just for a little ride.

Perhaps Dobbins was right that the train was a harbinger, but of a different type than he meant. Perhaps the phantom train was warning the Crescent that there was rough track ahead for it.

Between 1902 and 1907 the hotel was sold for back taxes and then passed hands several times. No one seemed able to re-capture the grandure and majesty that the Crescent had once enjoyed. The hotel was just as lovely and there were still as many reasons to come to the Crescent Hotel, but it could not be run profitably.

In 1908 the owners of the Crescent Hotel had been facing financial problems. The hotel was no longer receiving tens of thousands of visitors each year as it once had. The Frisco Railroad System did not want to lease it again and the owners needed a new source of revenue to keep the grand Crescent afloat in the off season.

The idea was proposed that a school should be opened at the Crescent during the off season which would cater to the children of some of the richest families in America.

The first term of the Crescent College And Conservatory For Young Women opened in September 1908. From September through the beginning of June the Crescent Hotel now doubled as a school, but in the summer months the hotel recaptured some of it's former glory by taking in guests once more.

During the hotels years as a school the young women who attended were not above a bit of foolery with the local lads. They would capture the eyes and attentions of local boys and convince them that they were in love. Some of the dalliances were more serious than others, but on the whole it was just a bit of fun the girls were out for.

The young ladies of the Junior College were also adventurous and creative. They convinced the young local men that they could come up to see the girls. Of course, the head master would never allow such a thing, so the girls devised a plan to surreptitiously allow their bows access to their bedrooms. It was agreed upon that the young ladies would lower a large basket they kept hidden when they heard the boys whistle below a certain balcony. The young ladies would then hoist the basket up and one by one the young men would gain entrance.

This worked well for a long while but at last stories of the illicit visits began to reach the ears of the college president, Mr. Richard R. Thompson who decided to put an end to the girls' shenanigans. One evening Mr. Thompson sauntered up to the balcony and gave the whistle for the girls to lower the basket. To the girls above the man below them appeared to be one of the local boys as Mr. Thompson was young and good looking and it was getting quite dark.

The young ladies lowered the basket and President Thompson stepped in. The young women began pulling the basket up and nearly had it to the top when they suddenly realized that the local lad was none other than President Thompson; they had been found out. In a vain attempt to escape punishment, the girls dropped the rope and the president, basket and all, tumbled to the ground below where he lay for a bit with the wind knocked out of him. The incident was quite amusing but there was another story generated during the Crescent Hotel's years as a college which was not nearly as pleasant.

The spirit of a young lady is said to haunt the fourth floor of the hotel. This young woman is dressed in early 1900's attire and she is often seen in the halls and rooms of the fourth floor where it is said she died.

Local newspapers today report the story as that she was one of the students who actually fell deeply in love with a local boy. There was a row when the relationship was discovered and the young woman either fell or jumped from the fourth floor balcony where the young men had so often come and gone. June Westphal told me a slightly different story about the young woman's demise. She had heard that the young man was faithless and had abandoned the girl. In despair the girl simply began to wither away. She grew ill and died in a room on the fourth floor of a broken heart. Ms. Westphal said that she had heard that the young woman appears in a long white dress and is seen only in the garden, the arcade and along the summer walk. Is this the spirit of the school girl or is there another young woman who haunts these areas? With a history like that of the Crescent Hotel, one can only speculate upon such things.

Today many guests of the fourth floor have seen her or felt her presence. The school girl is very timid and always quickly disappears when approached.

There have been reports of moving cold spots on the fourth floor, and it is reported by the hotel staff that they rarely put guests with pets on that floor as the animals seem to get agitated and frightened.

Long-time hotel manager, Jack Moyer, once gave an interview to a local newspaper in which he was quoted as saying, "Our owner's dog behaves very uncharacteristically on the fourth floor." He said that the normally quiet animal becomes "very agitated on that floor of the hotel."

After the college closed down at the end of the 1932 school year, the Crescent Hotel was run as a seasonal hotel for several years which meant that it was shut down for a good part of the year. Eventually it was sold to a Dr. Norman Baker who turned it into the Baker Hospital at a cost of $50,000.

This was perhaps one of the strangest and most controversial periods in the hotel's history. It seemed that there was much about the new hospital that made no sense. Dr. Baker was not a doctor (but he did have doctors on staff) and many of his claims were fantastic.

In 1937 Dr. Norman Baker opened a cancer hospital where he claimed he could help those with the dreaded disease. By combining large does of that "healing " spring water along with his therapy he claimed great success. His treatments were not cheap and only the affluent could afford the Baker treatment. Within three years Baker Hospital would be closed and Dr. Baker would be in prison in Leavenworth, Kansas for mail fraud. The mail fraud charges were leveled upon him because he had taken out advertisements for "cures" for cancer. The government claimed that he had no proof that his "cure" could help people with cancer in any form.

With the closing of the hospital, stories drifted down the mountain about the hospital and Dr. Baker's practices. Dr. Baker was variously a saint or a "mad scientist" depending upon who told the tale. He was accused of experimenting upon his patients by some, but others claimed that he helped and believed that Dr. Baker was a man much maligned. Other folks told tales of the hospital morgue in the basement. Today it is used for storage but does still exist.

Dr. Baker did not die in prison, as some claim. He apparently spent his final years in Florida, but he never made real peace with his destruction. Perhaps that is why his spirit has occasionally been seen in the Crescent Hotel. His ghost is an infrequent visitor but one of his staff still walks the halls and is seen more often.

Through the years many folks have reported seeing a nurse in 1930's uniform pushing a gurney or an old man in a wheel chair or a medicine cart. In an article which appeared in *THE FLASHPOINT*, August 1992, about the Crescent Hotel an hotel employee reports, "'...One woman who was staying here last year, and who didn't know the history of the hotel, came down one morning to check out and told us we had some employees who really worked late. She had gotten up at two-thirty in the morning to get some ice and saw a woman pushing a cart.' Needless to say, no Crescent Hotel employee pushes a cart (gurney?) down the hallways in the middle of the night."

There is one last little piece of lore about Dr. Baker which needs told. In 1973 a cat came to live at the Crescent Hotel. He went by the moniker of Morris and through the years some people came to believe that the cat was the reincarnation of Dr. Baker. Why I don't know, but even as Morris his tenure at the Crescent is long over again, I can't believe that the ancient beast still exists. One does wonder, though, if now Morris has joined the haunting?

Today Martin and Else Roenigk, a Connecticut couple, own the Crescent which they purchased in 1997. They have great respect for the history of this lovely hotel. They admire the classic architecture and want their guests to experience the Crescent as she was in her first heyday. There has long been a legend associated with the Crescent Hotel that it is protected by guardian angels who keep it safe. If that is true, then the angels must have led the Roenigks to the Crescent. They have given the Crescent a new lease on life, and it is well worth the trip to the Crescent just to experience the history or grandure of the majestic old lady of the Ozarks. There was no other hotel like the

Crescent in 1890, and today the Crescent is even more unique. There are only a few hotels the United States where you can experience the luxury of a bygone era.

If, however, you want to visit the Crescent for the ghosts, please remember that there are other guests who don't want to know about ghosts. Be quiet and just observe; it seems that the ghosts of the Crescent are timid and they don't appear to those seeking them.

THE PATROL

Douglas Prindle knew that things weren't always what they seemed. He remembered an evening when he and his kid sister, Loris were riding in his red Radio Flyer wagon near his Grandma's house. Grandma lived near the huge, fenced-in Union Cemetery in Milwaukee, Wisconsin, and as children, a cemetery was a fascinating place. That evening Doug and Loris saw something "rise" from one of the graves in the cemetery. Doug wanted to turn around but he could not let Loris know he was frightened, so he forced himself to continue toward the vast rows of tombstones. As he neared them, relief washed over him. The terrible spirit rising from the graves was only steam rising from a temporary pipe while the road near the cemetery was being repaired.

That night in Milwaukee taught Doug a lesson about jumping to conclusions and another lesson in ghosts--there weren't any. He became the most skeptical person around. Every ghost story had a simple explanation, but that was before Doug went to war and that was before Doug Prindle learned first hand that dead men can still walk.

When Doug was 22 years-old he was sent to Europe during W.W.II. He arrived as part of the Seventh Army and then was transferred to the third Army. He heard a few incredible stories along the way but Doug's logical mind stubbornly refused to accept any of that nonsense. Logic and reason were necessary features in his life and he literally depended upon them to keep himself alive, but it was getting harder and harder for Doug to find reasonable explanations for unusual events.

Once Doug was assigned to guard an outpost along the Rhine River alone. It was a dark night and even with his .50-caliber machine gun mounted on his jeep, his "liberated" side arm and his Army issued carbine, he felt a bit insecure. Doug kept wondering why he had been assigned the outpost alone; it was standard procedure to assign two men to each outpost. Two men could keep watch better than one, except that night.

As the darkness pressed against Doug, fear twisted his belly. He imagined he heard German voices in the whispering of the river and he thought German soldiers were nearby. When he was relieved, Doug felt both relief and shame. He had been falling apart out there. Never again, he vowed, would he allow imagination to rule his mind.

Throughout the many weeks that followed, Doug would see good men go a little crazy with the crawling fear of darkness and death. A fellow soldier, Hank, imagined that Germans were digging in the distance and tried to open fire. Had Doug not stopped him, Hank would have shot a tree--and allowed the Germans to know their exact position.

A few months later Doug was transferred to Troop A, 94th Reconnaissance Squadron (Mechanized) of the Fourteenth Armored Division. He was a private first class under the command of Seventh Army General Alexander Patch. (A unit that would later be commanded by General George S. Patton Jr. of the Third Army.)

Doug would later write:

"We had been trained in the States to find the enemy whenever contact was broken. One of the many rules of warfare is to always know the location of your adversary. Our job, however, was not to engage the enemy unless it was necessary to escape with information required by the brass. Our informal rule was to "sneak and peek."

"As all military personnel know, though, the rules often fly out the window when the shooting starts. Thus Troop A, on more than one occasion was committed ("volunteered by the colonel," we used to say) as infantry. And that's when we suffered the most casualties.

"It was a dark, cold, wintry night in France that two of our jeeps (we called them "peeps," because that was the term used only in armored divisions for those vehicles -- but I never learned why) and their crews were ordered by our captain to tour a certain area to "neutralize" German paratroopers. Word had come down from division that enemy soldiers had been dropped near our positions. We took "neutralize" to mean kill the person -- although that had not been spelled out.

"Our route took us through small farming communities. Without a doubt, the two of us in the first peep, and the trio in the vehicle behind, were glad that nothing was stirring. As on every other night in France, wooden shutters on the houses were closed, to discourage prying eyes and every other unwanted attention, including artillery barrages. The only noise came from our engines and the crunching of snow under the wheels. Talk was kept at a minimum.

"As we approached the center of one village, I saw what appeared to be a figure with a flowing cape running -- almost floating -- silently to our right. Not a sound came from footsteps or cape, or whatever it was -- perhaps a parachute? I watched as the figure darted into a tiny church cemetery.

"Was it the memories of the fellow "digging" and the enemy "talking" in the woods on the Rhine that prevented me from shouting out what I had seen? Indeed, had I really seen someone or something "floating" silently into a graveyard? I decided to say nothing to the driver, Sgt. Paul R. Shotola, who was continuing on, as was the peep behind us.

"But after no more than 50 feet of travel, I blurted to Shotola, "Did you see that guy running down the street just now?" Screech went the brakes, with Shotola demanding, "Did you see him too?" The guys in the peep behind us wanted to know what was up. They had seen nothing unusual.

"Both peeps were backed up beside the cemetery, which was the front yard of a small, ancient church. Shotola and I entered the church yard, which was surrounded by a wrought iron fence. The three other men remained with their peep on the road, expecting action.

"Check behind every gravestone," I whispered to Shotola, "but be damn careful." Our carbines were at the ready. It took only seconds to cover the graveyard, as it was so small. We figured no one entered the church, because the door was locked securely. The fence was too high and covered with winter-dormant growth, for an intruder to mount it quietly and not be seen by our guys in the other peep. Only Shotola's and my footprints disturbed the snow in the churchyard.

"Where had our quarry gone? No one said it, but I'm sure we five troopers had no doubt as to what the object was -- a real, live ghost, not a German soldier dragging his parachute.

"For years after the war, and before my son, Jeff, left for the next, he would bring friends home and demand, "Dad, tell that story about the ghost you saw in France!" Neither daughter, Nancy nor my late wife Marijayne wanted to hear it more than once, though.

"It's rare these days that I repeat this true tale. It's not at all rare, however, that it still mystifies me. Of course, rational me, I'm a non-believer in things spooky, but then....."

(I'm greatly indebted to Mr. Prindle for sharing his story with me. I know that I could not have told his story better than he did, so I'll just leave it in his own words, but I must admit that now I, too, am mystified as to what he and Shotola chased into a cemetery that night!)

THE MANY HAUNTS AT HEATHROW

Heathrow International Airport in England is indeed a very busy place. Nowhere in the world is there more hustle and bustle than at this huge airport. It is, therefore, very interesting that such a busy place is the home of several hauntings and, more importantly, so haunted that folks actually notice the ghosts.

Perhaps the oldest spirit at Heathrow actually pre-dates the airport being built. The spirit of legendary highwayman Dick Turpin has been seen. Turpin was a popular highwayman during the 1730's in England. He robbed, stole livestock and murdered for more than twelve years before he was hung in 1739. Turpin was popular with the poor folk because he focused upon robbing the wealthy and they enjoyed seeing the wealthy get their comeuppance.

In reality Turpin was a cruel man who reputedly set people on fire alive, raped and tortured female captives and once even dragged an old woman to death on his horse. He was a greedy man who cared little who he robbed, but his death insured that his legend would live on. Supposedly he approached his gallows with a swagger and a smile. He bowed with courtly charm to the beautiful young women who had come to see him hung. He then literally jumped from the ladder which supported him and hung himself. His bravado struck the common people and they quickly stole his body and buried it in quicklime so that it could not be given to the doctors to dissect.

Turpin's spirit has been seen throughout England, particularly along the A1 highway. Turpin has also been reported along the B488 near Woughton-on-the-Green, the A11, the A5 between Nuneaton and Hinckley, but he is most often seen near Hounslow Heath where Heathrow International Airport is. Turpin's spirit is as colorful as Turpin was in life. He reportedly wears a jacket with blood red sleeves, a black tri-corn hat, a black cloak and high boots. He rides upon a large black stallion, and has been seen galloping down many a country lane.

At Heathrow, though, Dick is not seen riding madly upon his black steed. Instead he is seen, heard or felt behind people. Employees of the airline, in particular, report feeling as though someone is behind them. They feel hot breath upon their necks and hear a man barking like a dog and howling. The employee then turns quickly and is most startled to find that there is not a living soul behind him. By all accounts, Dick Turpin enjoyed playing unnerving jokes like this in life and he's still doing so in death.

But there are more conventional spirits haunting Heathrow as well.

It is an unfortunate fact that most airports have had their tragic landings. Weather, mechanical failure and human error have taken a toll, and there have been terrible plane crashes in the history of Heathrow International Airport.

In 1948 a DC3 Dakota plane from Belgian Airlines crashed while on approach to Runway 2-8-Right during a terrible, foggy night. It was a horrible accident and no one survived. The British rescue crew worked feverishly to pull the victims from the twisted wreckage but they knew that there was no hope. As the men worked, a gentleman in a hat appeared in the fog and asked the workers if they had found his briefcase in the wreckage. He took the men by surprise and just faded away as they stared at him. According to the workers they later found the man's body in the wreckage.

Since that terrible night the man has been seen many times along the runway where he died so long ago. By most accounts he simply appears out of nowhere and walks along the runway as if searching for his briefcase still. Others say he appears confused or dazed as he wanders along. Could it be that he doesn't quite realize that he's dead and is still trying to complete whatever business deal brought him to England back in 1948?

There is yet another businessman who haunts the airport. This spirit is of a businessman in a gray suit who seems harried and worried. He haunts one of the VIP Lounges in the airport and simply materializes at odd moments. A few people have claimed to see him materialize only from the waist down. They are obviously disconcerted to see a pair of gray clad legs walking around the lounge.

Are there other spirits at Heathrow International Airport? In a place so busy and filled with people hurrying to various destinations it is hard to tell, but these three spirits have been so dedicated in their haunting that they have been noticed amidst the hubbub. So if you're traveling through Heathrow, keep your eyes open and you, too, might see a spirit passing through or a man in a hurry who just disappears before he can fade into the crowds.

THE CURSE ABOARD THE TITANIC

There are those people who would say the *R.M.S. Titanic* was doomed to sink. The ship was commonly labeled as "unsinkable" when notices of it's launching were published. It was the most amazing luxury ship to have ever graced the waters, but to say it was "unsinkable" was nothing short of tempting God or fate! Perhaps it's fate was sealed by the egotism of the builders and the White Star Line which owned the ship, but there are things about the *R.M.S. Titanic* which would not be known for quite some time. There would be stories of coincidences and ironic events, and of an Egyptian curse which might have sealed the real fate of the *R.M.S. Titanic*.

There has long been a story that the White Star Line had sunk a ship named *Titanic* while the real ship was being built. They deliberately did so to collect upon the large insurance policy attached to the vessel in order to continue work on the large luxury liner. That would mean that the *R.M.S. Titanic* was listed as sunk long before the actual disaster.

There are other stories about the destiny of *R.M.S. Titanic* which have much more validity. Author Morgan Robertson, in a novel he wrote in 1898 as a young writer, told the story of a 70,000 ton ship which was struck by an iceberg in the Atlantic ocean during its maiden voyage. This ship did not have adequate lifeboats and half the 2,500 passengers were lost because of this gross oversight. In his novel, Robertson stated that the large liner was equipped with only 24 lifeboats, and he described the terrible agony of decision making as women and children were placed aboard the tiny vessels by men who would soon die. The horrible fate that would befall the *R.M.S. Titanic* was described in nearly perfect detail. He wrote of the people perishing upon the freezing iceberg when they tried to climb onto it and were instantly stuck there alive. He described accurately the fate of those aboard who ended their lives in the icy water on a cold night. Perhaps the most amazing thing about Robertson's story was that he named his ill-fated ship the *R.M.S. Titan*. Were the fates trying to warn us to beware of such a ship?

If they were trying to warn us, they must have been terribly disappointed when on April 14, 1912 the real *R.M.S. Titanic* went down on her maiden voyage. She had only 20 lifeboats aboard; again less than half the amount needed. There were 2,224 passengers aboard this ship that night and 1,513 of those died. Was it an amazing coincidence, or had it been an unheeded warning from beyond?

In the early 1900's, several years before the shipping disaster, a London newspaper editor, W. T. Stead wrote, after reading Robertson's work of fiction, "This is exactly what might take place, and what will take place, if liners are sent to sea short of boats." Stead should have paid more attention to his own warning, for he would die in the icy waters of the Atlantic on April 14th, 1912. He had been a passenger aboard the *R.M.S. Titanic*.

Many people would call these stories predicting the fate of the *R.M.S. Titanic* as just coincidence, but how many coincidences does one shrug off? When do coincidences become prophetic warnings? Consider the last story of a passenger aboard this ill-fated vessel.

Douglas Murray, a debonair man, was not superstitious. Superstition was reserved for those who needed a reason not to live life, and Murray, only 48 years old, wanted to live life to the fullest. He was a wealthy man with a passion for archeology--especially

Egyptian archeology. Murray had worked as a talented amateur in the field for years and had a good reputation which was well deserved.

In 1910 Murray was working in Cairo, Egypt excavating a hill fort near the historic city of Thebes. He believed that this site had links to the Biblical story of the Jewish Exodus from Egypt, and he was determined to prove his theory was accurate.

Murray went to the bar in the hotel he was staying at one afternoon for a drink while he worked on his research notes. A young American man came up and asked Murray if he would buy "a fellow American" a drink. Murray looked up and was shocked to see that this fellow was surely sick. Though his looks still were in tact, he was quite obviously very ill. Murray told the fellow that he was English, but he would certainly buy him a drink.

The American sat down and accepted his drink. Murray was a bit annoyed for he had wanted to work on his notes. "I'm called Starbuck and you're Doug Murray, aren't you?" the fellow asked.

Murray accented but tried to indicate his notes.

"I know you, you're that archeologist, right?" Starbuck persisted.

Again Murray agreed, but told the American that he was only an amateur. Murray insisted that he had no degrees or formal training, but the American knew of Murray's reputation.

"No matter," Starbuck went on. "I have something you might like to buy."

By now Murray knew that he would not be able to return to his notes until he dealt with the persistent American.

"I'm afraid that I'm not looking to buy any artifacts right now..." Murray paused when his companion slumped forward toward the table. Again he was struck by this man's illness. Beneath his rugged features this man was wasted away. What type of illness would do that? He must have been sick for a long time to look so very bad.

"This is something you'll be willing to pay for once you see it, Mr. Murray," the American insisted.

"Well, what do you have, Mr. Starbuck?" Murray knew he'd have to look at whatever second-rate relic this fellow pulled from his pocket.

"What I have's not here. It's too big to carry. You'll need to come see it. This thing is really something..." Starbuck seemed to be pleading with Murray.

"If it's something important, why don't you keep it?" Murray asked.

Starbuck pinned Murray with his sickly gaze. "I'm dying and I know it. I'm from Missouri and I just want to go back home before I'm dead."

"Surely it's not that bad," Murray insisted in a comforting manner. "Perhaps if you get some rest and the proper medical treatment you'll be fine."

"I'm not fooling myself, Mister," Starbuck insisted. "I've got a fever of some kind and a bullet festering in my leg. I just want to go home to a Christian place to die."

Murray was impressed by the simple truth of the American's words. He felt his resolve not to buy whatever the American showed him waver. Perhaps he could buy the artifact for just enough money to get the poor fellow home.

The men talked a few more minutes before Starbuck wrote down his address on a scrap of paper. He pushed it across the table to Murray and cryptically muttered. "You meet me there at midnight, and you come alone!" With that the man stood up and hurried away on unsteady legs.

Murray looked at the address and felt some doubts. It was an area of warehouses in a rough part of Cairo. Perhaps he was being set up to be robbed or worse, but when the time came Murray went to the address and found Starbuck.

Starbuck let him into a dingy room with only one overhead light bulb to pierce the darkness. Within that pool of greasy yellow light there lay a case which Starbuck led Murray to.

"Mr. Murray, I'd like to introduce you to Princess Taheb." With a small flourish Starbuck pushed the lid from the case to reveal a figure. As he struggled with the lid, he collapsed into a coughing fit but he bushed away Murray's help. "Look at the Princess," he gasped. "She was most beloved by her subjects of the Nile. A Princess of Nubia and the Cataracts, she was Priestess of Ammon-ra at the great temple and High Priestess of the Cult of the Dead." With that Starbuck brayed a burst of laughter which chilled Murray.

"Ironic, isn't it?" the American demanded. "High Priestess of the Cult of the Dead, and she's about to come to collect another dead man."

Murray knew that Starbuck was speaking of himself but he didn't reply. His eyes were fastened to the gray face of the figure. It was a mummy of exquisite workmanship. She was breathtaking to him and he turned back to Starbuck. "How much?" he demanded.

"A thousand pounds and she's yours." Starbuck held up a hand when Murray tried to interrupt to tell him that such an artifact was worth much more. "I know she's worth more, but that's all I need. It will buy me passage home and a tombstone. Take it or leave it, Mr. Murray."

Exhausted from his efforts Starbuck sagged to the floor beside the box and leaned his head heavily against it.
"I'll take her, but you do realize that such a find is priceless, don't you?" Murray was a fair man.

"Not to me," Starbuck muttered. "Consider this your lucky day, Mr. Murray."

Murray wrote out a check and made arrangements for the immediate removal of the mummy. Murray would later learn that the check was never cashed. He inquired about Starbuck and learned that a Jonathan Starbuck of Missouri in the United States had died later that same evening and had been buried in Cairo. Starbuck had only been 27 years old and had been a soldier of fortune in Egypt until his illness struck. Murray could not help feeling sorry for the fellow who never got to return to his Missouri home to die.

Murray, though, had other things to worry about. He now needed to make secret arrangements to take his princess home to England. It was illegal to remove Egyptian artifacts from native soil, but for a price anything could be done.

Murray turned to a friend of his who was also an archeologist specializing in Egyptian history in order to get Princess Taheb shipped back to Sussex, England. His friend, however, was not surprised by Murray's story about Starbuck.

"You do know the history of your little princess, don't you?" his friend inquired.

"Not yet," Murray said, "But I intend to know her well before this is done."
His friend smiled at him cryptically. "Well let me help you. Princess Taheb was a high priestess in the Cult of the Dead and they believed that they would be resurrected from death to serve their Pharaoh and their many gods in the nether world. Furthermore, your princess has a curse attached to her. Anyone who disturbs her will find horror and sorrow. I believe that the curse also applies to those who defile her tomb or who touch her body."

Murray smiled. "Perhaps that's what got Starbuck." He laughed. "But this priestess and I will be great friends. She'll not bother me." Murray was surprised at the fellow scientist's superstitious words.

A box containing the princess was shipped to England and three days later Murray was badly injured during a hippopotamus hunt on the Nile. His perfectly functional rifle suddenly exploded in his hands. Murray would ultimately loose his right arm when gangrene was found in the wound. This devastated Murray and he returned to Sussex in many respects a broken man.

The archeologist friend who had helped surreptitiously ship out the princess died aboard the ship that carried him home. His death was never explained as no cause could be found. The two assistants who had carried the mummy aboard the ship were drowned when they were swept overboard during a storm.

Murray had become a believer in Princess Taheb's vengeful curse. He wanted only to be rid of the horrid mummy. He would die only two years after returning to Sussex, and on his deathbed he confessed that he had been terrified of the mummy. He said that when he unpacked her she seemed to smile at him in a way that chilled his bones.

Murray did get rid of the princess but only after much persuasion, and then with great trepidation. A lady friend of his, who was a member of the British Royal family, saw the mummy and insisted upon having it. At first Murray refused for fear the curse would turn upon her, but at last he acquiesced and she took possession of the mummy.

Murray was loath to find out that only weeks later this woman's mother died, her lover was found to be having affairs with many other men and women and that he was ill with a wasting disease (probably AIDS) which she also contracted. She died a horrible death.

This woman in her will sent the cursed object she blamed for her own demise back to Murray, but he was frightened of the mummy. Poor Murray had not had a pleasant time of it after purchasing Princess Taheb and he feared her now. He donated the mummy to the British Museum which accepted her. Curators there believed that curses were all in the mind. However, Princess Taheb would make her presence known at this prestigious museum.

The first life she claimed at the museum was that of a photographer who did the photographs for a London newspaper. Coming out of the museum after taking photographs of Princess Taheb, he died of a heart attack on the museum steps.

By now the public was interested in Princess Taheb. She was a colorful figure with a vengeful streak which caught the imagination of the public.

The mummy was being considered by the board of directors at the museum as a part of their permanent Egyptian display. The man in charge of this investigation was found dead in his bed before a decision could be reached.

The board of directors were troubled by the reputation the mummy was getting. They did not believe in curses, at least not publicly, but the curse associated with this mummy might hurt the museum, so they unanimously voted to offer the mummy to a New York museum. The whole matter was very quietly done. Perhaps the mummy would no longer be cursed after she crossed the Atlantic.

The New York museum had only one requirement, they wanted the mummy transported across the Atlantic in the safest possible way in order to belie the rumors of a curse. The curators of the British Museum hit upon the very thing. A new "unsinkable" ship was about to leave Southampton on its maiden voyage to New York. This great ship of the White Star Line could carry Princess Taheb safely to American shores and end the story of a curse.

Quietly the mummy was loaded aboard the ship hidden in a wooden crate and was stowed in a small baggage area behind the command bridge. The British Museum was satisfied that now they had outsmarted the idea of a curse. This ship was built using the best technology available and everyone agreed it was "unsinkable." Princess Taheb would quietly reach America now.

Princess Taheb, however, never completed her voyage as did another nearly fifteen hundred people. She went down when the R.M.S. *Titanic* sunk in the early morning hours of April 15. Some survivors would forever criticize the experienced ship's captain, Edward J. Smith, for his odd actions upon the ship's maiden voyage. They claimed that Capt. Smith plotted an erratic course and moved the vessel along at speeds clearly too fast for the prevailing conditions. They said the captain acted "odd" and seemed vague in the days prior to the ship's sinking. Furthermore, after the ship collided with the iceberg the captain waited until the last moments to announce a rescue plan. Had he immediately set a plan in action perhaps more people would have survived.

Other people blamed the owner of the White Star Line, Mr. Ismay, who wanted the ship to arrive in New York on time, and people claimed he forced Capt. Smith to go against his better judgment. Perhaps that was true, but there is also one other possible explanation...

In 1989 American Egyptologist Ken Weeks, working in The Valley of the Kings, found the entrance to a tomb dubbed KB-5. Inside this tomb around forty of the princely sons of Ramesses II were buried. The Egyptologist noticed something about the tomb; there was fungus growing on the walls. Subsequently, through the efforts of several prominent scientists, it has been discovered that a deadly form of fungus known as Aspergillus Niger often grows inside tombs. The conditions inside a tomb are perfect for this fungus. A dark, damp place with lot of food in the form of the vegetable dyes used in paints and the plant offerings to the dead royal leader would feed many generations of this fungus. It has been theorized that if anything did mysteriously kill some of those who would work in King Tutankhamun's tomb fifteen years later, it was a fungus spore they breathed in and not a mummy's curse.

Aspergillus Niger can make one ill and the symptoms can appear like a case of pneumonia, but others have speculated that it can also affect the body so that memory and judgment are altered. Is it possible that Captain Smith breathed in these spores while in the command bridge every day, and that this affected his judgment? No one will ever know for sure, but mummy's curse or fatal fungus, there was some force seemingly at work to destroy that vessel. Perhaps is was only the arrogance of mankind that caused God to allow such a tragedy, or perhaps a mummy did reach out from beyond the grave to stop those who defiled her and find herself a permanent tomb where the curious could not disturb her peace.

In a bizarre postscript to the terrible *Titanic* story at least one person has attributed a lifesaving premonition to the spirits of those who died in the waters and aboard the ship, R.M.S. *Titanic*.

On April 13, 1935 William Reeves was lookout aboard a steamer named *Titanian*, which was crossing the north Atlantic. He was reading Morgan Robertson's book *Futility* about the mythical R.M.S. *Titan*. About an hour before midnight Reeves was in his cabin reading the book when suddenly he felt a keen awareness of the similarity between his own situation and that of the ship in the book. Reeves tried to shrug off the feeling but by 11:30 it was nearly impossible.

At 11:35 p.m., the time when the R.M.S. *Titanic* had been struck, Reeves suddenly had a terrible sense of danger. He began thinking about the R.M.S. *Titanic* which had met it's fate in the same waters he now plied. A terrible feeling of great danger overcame him and he hurried to the lookout's post. Despite seeing nothing which should have alarmed him, Reeves was now terribly frightened. He called to stop the ship with a cry of, "Stop engines, now! Iceberg ahead!"

The ship came to an abrupt stop and suddenly Reeves and other crewmen saw what had not been visible only seconds before. A huge iceberg loomed up before them in their path. The iceberg did slightly damage the *Titanian*, but it would have been a much worse situation if they had driven directly into it. Reeves, when questioned about his strange actions which saved both the ship and crew, insisted that the spirits of the poor *Titanic* passengers had given him a premonition so that another ship would not suffer their fate!

While doing the research upon this story, I contacted the Titanic Historical Society which wrote back insisting that there was no mummy aboard the Titanic and that this whole story was a hoax. I understand that this group is dedicated to preserving the story of the Titanic and in commemorating those many lives lost. It is possible that they feel this story does some disservice to the memory of so many, but I do not believe that. There has been enough other documentation to make me believe that I could present this story accurately. However, I want the Titanic Historical Society's letter on the record, too. I also want to assure them and anyone else who might take exception to this story, that I have great respect for the memory of those lost on the S.S. Titanic. No single act by anyone could possibly taint the sacrifice and tragedy surrounding the worst nautical disaster in history.

STONE COLD SPIRITS

When I was a teenager, I used to have a recurring nightmare about a local cemetery near my high school. An alley cut the cemetery in half so that one had to walk through it to go into the alley. I rarely took this route because it was out of my way, but this particular alley began to haunt my dreams. I dreamt that I was watching a pretty woman with light brown hair who wore a long dress and coat. It was a cold, gray January day with sleet spitting and an icy wind blowing. The woman was walking through the alley when she heard the thin, pained wails of an infant. She winced at the very idea of a baby being out on such a cold day. The cries were terrible and she began looking for the baby. She turned and opened the right side gate. There she saw a chubby infant laying naked upon the dead grass on the frozen ground before a tombstone. The child squirmed and wiggled it's arms and feet as it cried in protest against the cold that bit at it. Who could be so terribly cruel? As she touched the child, it's pale, translucent skin turned the gray of granite and the living baby turned to stone beneath her fingers. It still moved, but now she could not touch the cold stone baby. Her screams always awoke me. Perhaps that was why I began collecting stories of cold stone which seemed imbued with the ability to move. In fact, there is a whole legion of funeral statues which have come to be known commonly as "Black Aggie's." These pieces are usually of women or angels and have earned their reputation as haunted through many years. Here are a few of the not so still statues I've collected the stories about during my many years of searching

THE LITTLE GUARD DOG

On Cherry Street in Richmond, Virginia there is the Hollywood Cemetery. This cemetery has long been believed to be haunted by several entities. Terrible moans are reported emanating from a great stone pyramid which was erected over the mass grave of eighteen thousand Civil War soldiers who were mostly buried without their identity being known.

Writer Ellen Glasgow was buried in Hollywood Cemetery along with her two beloved dogs in 1945. People have reported hearing her dogs barking when they approach her grave.

But the most tragic and mysterious haunting in Hollywood Cemetery is that of a little girl who's grave is eternally guarded by a small cast-iron dog. The little cast-iron dog stood outside the door of a store on Broad Street in Richmond and the child had always enjoyed playing with it. She never missed her opportunity to pet it each time she walked that street. The shop owner thought the child was charming and funny and he enjoyed watching her play with the iron dog. During the flu epidemic of 1892 the little girl passed away and the store owner gave the iron dog to the family for on the child's grave. This act of kindness seemed to give the little dog a special power for since that time visitors to the cemetery have occasionally come away unnerved by the cast-iron dog's behavior. It seems to "come alive," barking and growling if it senses that some one wishes to trespass upon his little mistress's peace.

THE BLACK ANGEL

Druid Ridge Cemetery in Pikesville, Maryland has long had a reputation for being badly haunted. The hauntings centered upon the grave sight of General Felix Angus, a newspaper publisher who was buried in the 1920's. Atop his headstone stood a black angel which quickly earned the cemetery it's reputation. It was first said that at midnight the eyes of the black angel glowed red at the midnight hour. People said that this black angel called forth the spirits of the dead in the cemetery and through her they could enter this world and haunt for just a few hours each night.

People began calling the angel "Black Aggie" and warned that if her glowing eyes fell upon you she would steal your sight. Pregnant women were warned to avoid her glowing gaze or she would cause them to miscarry. The local stories about "Black Aggie's" evil are legion.

Soon, though, "Black Aggie" became the focal point of a local college fraternity's initiation process. They would fill the pledge's head full of terrible stories about the black angel and her evil deeds before taking the pledge to Druid Ridge Cemetery. There they would leave him. If he survived the night, he had passed the test. Most times, the fellows would wait out the miserable night away from the Black Angel, but there is a story that once the pledge did not leave in time. During the test "Black Aggie's" eyes fell upon him and he died of fright.

Another story about the black angel dates from 1962 when a local man was arrested for damaging the statue. He was caught with a hack saw but he insisted that though he had gone to the cemetery to cut off one of the black angel's arms as a gag, he had not succeeded. In a shaken voice he said that "Black Aggie" had grabbed the saw and cut off her own arm. In terror he had grabbed up his saw and fled, no longer a skeptic. Though that story sounded quite ridiculous to the local police, the man never wavered in his assertion that "Black Aggie" came to life and cut off her own arm to frighten him.

By 1967 stories about the black angel were so popular that the cemetery was becoming a popular spot at night. So many people trampled through the cemetery that the directors decided "Black Aggie" had to go. They donated her to the Smithsonian Institution where she is to this day. Now she is part of a collection of statuary which the museum owns. Though the statue has never been displayed, Smithsonian officials did not say why.

THE WONDERING STATUE OF WILLIAM PENN

Pennsylvania is the birth place of democracy, and the city where that birthing occurred is Philadelphia. Here the founding fathers surreptitiously created a new nation and overthrew a dictator's rule. Here, also, are many other firsts. The first library, post office, fire station, and hospital are but a few of Philadelphia's many contributions to this nation. The oldest hospital in America should be haunted and it is, but not by a vengeful wraith or even a pathetic spirit mourning, but rather by the graceful wandering statue of the state's first white founder, William Penn.

Pennsylvania Hospital, located on Pine Street, has cared for many a prominent

American, and it has become more than just a hospital, it is a museum. On the first floor there are many valuable works such as a chair owned by William Penn and the actual first operating room in America.

The gardens of the hospital, too, are a place of great history. There you can walk the same ground as many a forefather, and a statue of the William Penn graces the lovely landscape. The statue was created most probably in the 1770's but it was not until John Penn, William's son, found it in a London salvage yard that it was sent to Philadelphia. In 1804 he donated the statue to Pennsylvania Hospital. There Penn's statue has stood and through the years a very strange story has grown up around it. William Penn's statue is said to step down from it's pedestal and walk around.

The first written mention of it appears in a letter from Benjamin Franklin to a friend. This letter was mentioned in an article in an issue of the Philadelphia Bulletin from 1905. The story of Penn's nightly walks seems to date back to just after it was erected in the hospital garden. Through the years nurses, security guards, and visitors to the hospital along with pedestrians passing by have claimed to see Penn step down and take a stroll. There seems to be no particular nights he prefers. Different versions of the tale make different claims. Some say he walks only on New Year's Eve, while others say that when the clock in Independence Hall struck six p.m. each evening Penn was called forth. Still another version claimed that only on the full moon each month did he wander the hospital grounds.

The Philadelphia Press printed an article about the wandering statue in 1884 in which they claimed that Penn's strolls were so numerous that, "Nurses brought children from afar to watch it."

There is yet another version of the story which says that people have witnessed Penn's statue walking along Pine Street. It is said that Penn's spirit is eternally tied to the statue and that he enjoys walking along his city of "Brotherly Love" from time to time. One can only speculate upon what poor William Penn thinks today when he sees the crime and poverty which has attached itself to some corners of his beautiful city. Perhaps, though, Penn has never wandered far enough afield to be disturbed by urban strife and inner city crime.

THE VANISHING STATUE OF GRACELAND

Today the name Graceland conjures up visions of Elvis Presley and his stately mansion, but Graceland is also the name of a cemetery in the Chicago, Illinois area. There stands the statue of a little girl in a ruffled dress with a hat and parasol who is sitting in her stone chair. The statue marks the grave of six-year-old Inez Clark who passed on in 1880. Little Inez was a beloved child and her parents' grief is understandable. The Clarks had a life-sized statue of Inez made to sit upon her grave. A year after it was finished it was placed inside a glass box so as to protect it from the weather. Inez can still be seen today sitting like a beautiful cherub with her pretty face barely touched by time.

Through the years a story has built up around the statue of Inez that she simply disappears from her grave at certain times. She seems to dislike thunderstorms and is often found gone during them. A guard at the cemetery years ago found Inez's glass case empty during a particularly terrible storm. He left the cemetery and never came back. Through the years other guards have also reported Inez missing only to have her mysteriously reappear when the authorities looked in the morning.

Through the years Inez has become very popular. People seem to grieve for the child who was lost so long ago. Her own family died out years ago, but Inez never lacks sympathetic visitors who bring the little stone ghost toys, flowers and other small treasures. Perhaps their efforts are meant to ease the long sojourn of the lonely little spirit in her stone temple.

"GRIEF"

One of the oddest stone statues was one commissioned by famed Harvard historian Henry Adams while he lived in the District of Columbia. Adams was an odd man who seemed to care little for his fragile young wife, Marian. During the 1880's the couple lived in Washington and Henry was greatly preoccupied by outside interests. Stories of young Marian's terrible loneliness would make the rounds of the local gossip mills after she was found dead before the fireplace in the living room of their home late one night by Henry. The circumstances of her death have remained unclear and the uncharitable said she committed suicide because of her husband's neglect.

Whatever caused Marian's death, Henry's reaction to it was nothing short of bizarre. He attended to the funeral arrangements, but ordered that her tombstone remain blank. He then commissioned sculptor Augustus Saint-Gaudens to make a bronze statue for his wife's grave that would not be "intelligible to the average mind." Saint-Gaurdens did more than he was asked to. He created a full-length bronze statue of a woman in a long veil. Something about the statue was quite disturbing and the commission in charge of the cemetery refused to have it erected. Henry Adams, though, lobbied them until they relented and the statue was put in place. Soon after it was erected people began complaining that a terrible sadness took them over when they viewed the statue. Others claimed to see a very frail woman looking up at the statue. When they approached closer, she simply vanished. Yet others claimed that the statue itself wept beneath the veil in terrible grief for all the dead. The statue locally was dubbed "Grief" and remains commonly known by that name today.

Adams went on to great prominence but he literally cut Marian from his history. He never mentioned her and never even admitted to being married. He even left Marian out of his memoirs when he wrote them years later. Marian's gravestone is still blank, but those who visit the cemetery will know it immediately because above it stands eternally "Grief."

THE MARBLE BALL

Throughout the Mid-Western United States there are monuments of huge marble balls which sit in granite bases. These are fairly common to that region and it would not be unique to see them in a cemetery, but in the Oak Hill cemetery in Taylorsville, Illinois there is a huge marble ball which does not want to stay put. Caretakers have noticed through the years that this ball which marks the Adams and Richardson plots has been rolling in it's base.

Starting in about 1910 the caretakers began to realize that the ball was rotating. When it was set in the granite base, the smooth marble was visible all around and the only rough spot was where the ball fit firmly into it's base. Through the years the ball has been rotating so that the rough spot is clearly visible now. The ball weighs many hundreds of pounds and is much too heavy for one, two or even three men to roll safely. The ball has slowly been moving for many years. What causes the ball to rotate is not known but some say that it's being done by a restless spirit which has taken up habitation in the stone sphere.

THE STONE SOLDIER

Vietnamese sculptor Nguyen Thanh Tu created the thirteen foot high bronze statue of a weary soldier sitting in a seat. The lonely, sad, battle worn man has a gun across his knees, his body is bowed with the weight of what he has seen and done and immediately the statue gives one a sense of exactly how this man must feel. Nguyen Thanh Tu called his statue "Sorrow," and this statue is a memorial erected in 1966 in the South Vietnamese military cemetery along the Saigon-Bienltoa highway.

Since shortly after this statue was erected stories of the thirteen-foot high man rising and walking have been told by the locals of the area. Many of the local people worship their ancestors, so it should not be surprising that they left offerings of food and wine at the foot of the statue which honored their dead. But when the locals returned all the rice and wine were gone, had the statue eaten them or had some wandering bum who took advantage of his lucky find?

Local people have claimed to see the bronze man get up and walk. They say he has tears steaming down his face as he cries for all soldiers lost in battle, no matter which side they fought for.

The Americans were still fighting in Vietnam in the late 1960's and for one unit of South Vietnamese soldiers the stories of the statue took on a whole new meaning. Late one night a gigantic figure stepped into the rutted road ahead of a 20-vehicle convoy which was traveling in the open. The gigantic bronze man stunned the soldiers. The bronze man held his massive gun over his head. "Go back! Ambush!" the figure cried. The convoy turned and retreated. These men believed not only that the statue had moved but that it had also saved their lives.

Many local people believe that the soldier walks and grieves for the many dead he has seen. They believe that until lasting peace comes to Vietnam the soldier will never rest. Many very reliable people such as military police officers and civilian police have reported seeing the statue step down and walk. One can only wander if "Sorrow" will ever find true peace in such a place?

BEN FRANKLIN'S DANCING STATUE

During his life Benjamin Franklin was celebrated as a genius, an inventor and a statesman, but Ben Franklin also had a reputation for being a bit "odd." Among the odd things Franklin did was take daily air baths. He would sit naked in his chambers and work. He claimed that human skin needed to breath so many hours a day in order to free itself of impurities. Considering Ben Franklin's reputation, it should surprise no one that

Benjamin Franklin's statue does not just move it supposedly dances.

According to a story dating back to the 1800's, the statue of Franklin which stood in a niche above the door of the Philadelphia Library would jump down and dance down the street each Easter morning. The old library located on South 5th Street is now called Library Hall and is owned by the American Philosophical Society. The statue of Ben Franklin which stands in the niche today is not the "dancing" statue. That statue was removed years ago and is now in storage at the library Company building at 1314 Locust Street. This statue was supposedly replaced because of its weathered condition, but some folks say it was removed because of Ben's habit of dancing to celebrate Easter morning.

Of course, the spirit of Ben Franklin is also said to haunt Philadelphia, but that is another story...

THE MAN WHO DID NOT WANT A MARKER

Perhaps one of the strangest stories of moving stone is that of the tall stone obelisk which marks the grave of Kentucky state judge John Rowin. Rowin died in 1843 and was a man much respected in his time. His body was buried in the Bardstown Cemetery but his family and friends refused to honor his requests concerning his grave site. Rowin had been a most influential man who had been Chief Justice for the court of appeals in Kentucky. He had spent seven terms in the state legislature and was a U.S. Senator as well as a judge. But Rowin was also a pragmatic man who expressly told his family he did not want a tombstone or any sort of marker over his grave. Still, it just seemed wrong that such an outstanding man not be remembered in death, so his family and friends decided to erect the tall stone over Rowin's grave.

Within two months of having the stone erected it was found laying down as though a very strong person had somehow pushed it over. The groundskeepers scratched their heads and returned the obelisk to it's proper position. A few weeks went by and again the stone was tipped over. It was once more righted. Again and again for nearly one hundred fifty years, the stone atop Rowin's grave has been knocked down. In the beginning skeptics said it was a joke while others said Rowin was pushing the thing over because he did not want it there. To this very day the standing stone occasionally is tipped. Is Rowin still angry about his wishes being ignored, or is there another reason that the stone can't stay firmly planted on the ground?

I have barely begun to scratch the surface of the subject of stone spirits and statues which somehow don't stay put. Many of the stories are legends, but even legends often have truth in them. Who knows? Maybe the human spirit is so strong that it can even make granite and bronze bend to its will!

THE RED GIRL OF HUNTINGTON COLLEGE

Nearly every college campus in the United States sports it's own ghost. From Gettysburg College in Pennsylvania with it's story of the Blue Boy to the many ghosts supposedly haunting Harvard College in Cambridge, Massachusetts, it just seems that the tumult and turmoil of college life is such that it leaves beyond many souls.

In Montgomery, Alabama there is the spirit of the Red Girl said to haunt Huntington College. The story of the girl who haunts Pratt Hall is sad and shows how cruelty can not only kill but devastate the spirit as well.

The date of the haunting is not known but it is believed that the story dates from the early 1900's. A young girl came to the college from New York to live on the fourth floor of Pratt Hall. This girl was painfully shy and this made her difficult to know. The girl, however, was desperately lonely and wanted friends.

Through the fall of that year the girl longed for friendship or a chance to go home. The other girls thought she was "weird" because she had a fascination for the color red and they fixed upon that as a way to make fun of her. The girl had red clothing, a red bedroom, red furniture and even red linens and blankets. It was easy to see how she could be called the "Red Girl."

At last the desperation and loneliness took a toll on the young girl. She decided that there was nothing for her to live for. Some accounts say she hung herself in her bedroom, while by other accounts she slit her wrists. She was found, they say, wearing a red nightie and robe, partially covered by a red blanket and laying in a pool of her own blood.

Since shortly after her death, girls at Pratt's Hall have encountered the spirit known as the Red Girl in the halls of the fourth floor. She is a terrifying sight with her red on red clothing and she had frightened many a student.

Several of the young women who have been given the room where the Red Girl died, have reported red flashing lights in the room for which they can find no source. Some girls have also reported that the Red Girl is still in her room. There have been reported sightings of her, chilled places, and even footsteps and a loud bang associated with the haunting. Some of the more sensitive young women who have stayed in the Red Girl's room have reported a terrible sense of loneliness and depression. Are they experiencing what that poor girl felt when she ended her life?

We tend to look back upon our youth as a wonderful time, but it can also be a time of unbearable cruelty and suffering for some people. It is not hard to imagine what the life of that poor girl must have been like, and it's no wonder that her soul has not yet found peace. Let's hope that in death she will find more acceptance than the living gave her.

WHAT WILL HAPPEN TO PHYLLIS PARKER?

1903

The middle-aged woman sat in rapt silence listening to the man on the podium speak. It was as though he was speaking to her alone. She clasped her hands tightly lest they tremble and tried to focus her attention upon the storyteller, Robert Breese, but it was difficult not to close her eyes. She was emotionally reliving an event from twenty-five years in her past. Robert Breese, storyteller, didn't know it, but he was providing an explanation to a mystery in her life that she had thought she had long forgotten. Now his words made everything clear again.

"There's a story that's been a part of the unofficial history of Vealtown," Robert Breese had begun, "But that does not make it untrue. I grew up in this town and I heard the tale directly from some of those who knew the folks involved.

Back during the Revolution, the house that's on what's now called Morristown Road, you know the one with the two chimneys and the old porch. Well that house was the Vealtown Tavern back in 1777 and a Captain Parker owned it. Downstairs was a taproom and a dining room and upstairs there were rooms for rent. Captain Parker was a widower with a teenage daughter named Phyllis. Phyllis was a lovely girl and she could have been no more than sixteen when she fell in love with a newcomer to the area who had taken up lodgings in the tavern. This fellow, Dr. Byram was a good-looking fellow and an excellent doctor.

Phyllis and the doctor kept company under the watchful and approving eye of Captain Parker. The Captain liked the doctor and he felt this was a good match for his daughter.

In late January there were important visitors to Vealtown. General Anthony Wayne came and took up lodgings. He and his troops were under the command of George Washington to deliver some very important dispatches. Wayne and his officers took up lodgings that night at the tavern and they drank and ate their fill. It was a raucous night of music and laughter by all accounts but, though Dr. Byram was present, he left early and went to bed.

When Captain Parker awoke the next morning, he was only mildly surprised to find that Dr. Byram and his horse were missing. He assumed, though, that the doctor must have been called out in the middle of the night as sometimes happened.

Downstairs Phyllis began breakfast for the prestigious men, but when General Wayne roused he sent a man downstairs to fetch Captain Parker.

Captain Parker found the General in a furious state of mind. "There's a spy in this neighborhood!" the General shouted at the surprised tavern keeper. "Several people have sent word of our being here to the British Army and only last month someone in this area gave away Lee's position and caused his capture, and now this... I've been commissioned to deliver a sensitive dispatch but it's been stolen. Some one here is a spy, I tell you!"

Poor Captain Parker, who had worked hard for the American cause, denied that such a thing could happen. He vehemently insisted, "I can not believe such a thing, sir. I know every man around here and they are all loyal local men and I've known them all of my life. There's only one fellow who is not from this area and I can personally vouch for him. In fact, sir, I trust this man so much that I allowed him to become betrothed to my own daughter!"

"Who is this man? What is his name? Describe him to me," General Wayne demanded.

Parker did not hesitate. "His name is Dr. Byram and he's got dark hair, a beard and is a good looking, friendly fellow."

General Wayne paused and looked sharply at the tavern keeper. "Do you have a picture of this man?"

Captain Parker assented. "Dr. Byram gave Phyllis a miniature of himself. Just a minute and I'll fetch it for you."

Within a few moments Captain Parker was back with the miniature which he handed to General Wayne.

Wayne studied the face intently and handed the miniature to an officer. "There is no doubt, do you agree. It is Aaron Wilde, the Tory spy! I recognize him despite his beard and long hair."

General Wayne ordered up his horse and readied the troops for there was no time to be lost. This spy must be caught before he delivered the dispatch.

As General Wayne rode off, Captain Parker decided to keep this news from his daughter. He knew Dr. Byram so well that despite the General's assurances that Byram was this spy named Wilde he could not believe it. Until Parker had proof he would not burden his daughter for he knew that she was deeply in love.

That bitterly cold day finally came to an end and Captain Parker had still not had any word of Dr. Byram's fate. Suddenly all of that changed when a local fellow named James Goble hurried into the tavern and insisted upon speaking with Captain Parker alone. He told Parker a story which chilled Parker's blood. Goble claimed that a Tory spy had been captured only a mile and a half away. The fellow had spoken to some of General Clinton's men in Basking Ridge at Mrs. White's Tavern. A soldier rode to tell General Wayne the whereabouts of the spy while the others remained behind to keep watch lest the spy slip away.

Wayne immediately set out after the spy with a force of men. En route to Basking Ridge he came upon the doctor at a place called Blazure's Corner. Immediately the doctor was seized and taken into the only house in the area. A search of the doctor's person gave damning testimony to the man's real identity and purpose in the area. A trial was held and the doctor was found guilty. General Wayne sentenced the man to be immediately hung and his order was immediately carried out posthaste.

Goble finished his tale in a hushed whisper. Before the hanging General Wayne gave the spy a chance to speak his last words. The doctor asked that he be allowed to write a letter to Phyllis whom he truly did care for and that Captain Parker might be sent word of his fate. He asked that Captain Parker, who was a good man, might take his body and give him a proper burial. General Wayne granted the Tory spy's requests, then he hung the spy.

Captain Parker was now in an agony of fear lest Phyllis find out the truth. He swore Goble to secrecy and instructed the servants and those who had heard Goble's story not to breath a word of it to poor Phyllis.

The Captain fabricated a reason to leave the tavern and hurried to Blazure's Corner where to his horror he found his friend and future son-in-law dangling from a tree. He enlisted help of some soldiers and together they cut down the doctor's body and Captain Parker made sure that the body was securely hidden in a coffin which he had personally seen was nailed shut.

Captain Parker, with the aid of some soldiers, brought the casket back to the tavern. He told Phyllis that the casket contained the body of a Tory spy who had been executed and that it would only be in the tavern for one night. Early the next morning the body would be buried.

Phyllis seemed content with her father's version of the story and retired for the night before the soldiers carried the casket into the dining room. They placed the box upon the floor and retired themselves. It had been a long, harrowing day for Captain Parker and he, too, fell gratefully into bed. In the morning he would face what had to be done but for now blessed slumber gave him some peace.

The night was cold and the people within the darkened tavern were grateful for the heavy quilts which protected them from the cold. They were loathe to leave the warm nests they inhabited and were not quite sure what sound startled them awake at first.

They listened as the quiet was torn by the sound of thumping as if someone hammered against wood; then came the sound of boards groaning and screeching in protest as they were pried up. Those who knew the tavern well quickly realized that the sounds came from the dining room below them.

As the listeners tried to make sense of the sounds they heard, another sound forever broke the quiet of the tavern. A terrible scream from below sent them all flying downstairs with lit candles and clutched bedclothes. In the dining room they found Phyllis kneeling beside the casket wailing and sobbing as she lay across the body of her dead love. A single candle lit the casket and shone upon the face of the dead doctor.

Captain Parker hurried forward and gently lifted his daughter up. A terrible sick shock clutched his heart as Phyllis's eyes met his. Gone was the intelligent, witty daughter he had adored, and in her place was a mad creature with eyes no longer touched by comprehension.

Phyllis was cared for the rest of her life by her father and his servants but never again did she laugh and smile. Never again did she dream of marriage and children. Never again would she delight her father with witty tales. Captain Parker had lost both his treasured friend and his daughter.

General Wayne was immediately informed of the incident with Phyllis by his soldiers who had witnessed her discovery of the body of the dead doctor. No one ever knew for sure how Phyllis had found out that it was her love in the casket or what had triggered her suspicions but General Wayne was horrified by the turn of events. In all ways this incident had been tragic and he ordered that no official record be kept of the incident. General Wayne was remorseful for his harsh and imprudent actions which had brought such devastation but there was nothing he could do to change things. A man was dead and his fiancee was insane. At least he could purge the records of all mention of this event, but the memory of the people of Vealtown was long and they did not forget. They told the story to their children and their children's children and it was never forgotten in the town.

The woman in the audience closed her eyes as she listened and remembered. It had been 1877, apparently the 100th anniversary of the night Phyllis had opened that casket when the lady had been left alone with her infant child in the house. The woman had not known about Phyllis or her tragic life. She only knew that the house made her feel uncomfortable and she had heard things...like skirts swishing by. Local rumor said that the house was haunted, but this lady had to live there and did not want to think of ghosts.

She remembered how cold the house was and how empty it felt that January night after her husband had left for Morristown on business. She remembered how terrified the sounds of rending boards in the middle of the night was. She recalled the sound of men walking; carrying something heavy across the porch and into the house through the kitchen door. She remembered also the terrible scream that ended the night.

Later the woman would tell her story to the local newspaper, the *Newark Sunday News* and the following appeared on February 22, 1903:

> I had resided in the old Vealtown Tavern over two years before the following occurrence, if such it can be called, took place. Prior to moving into the house, I had heard whispers of its being haunted, but as I was not at all superstitious, it never troubled me. The sounds we often heard at night of some one walking softly through the long halls, the swish of silken skirts against the banisters of the stairs, the raising of windows by invisible hands and the loud crash of their sudden falling, we always ascribed to rats or our imagination. I had really during those two years gotten quite used to such noises and thought they went with the house, and long before had decided not to let things I could not understand trouble me.
>
> They reached a climax, however, on a clear, cold, January night in the year 1877. It had been a dismal, dark day, with a promise of snow in the air. My husband had been called to Morristown on business and had told me to lock the house early as he would not be home before midnight. I remember it got dark early and I put my year-old baby to bed up-stairs in the old east room of the tavern. I had an open fire in the room and usually sat there evenings reading a book or sewing. With the door bolted, I felt safe and did not worry about the strange noises I heard coming from the hall and the attic.
>
> This evening however, I wanted to finish a dress I was making for my son. Since my sewing-machine was downstairs, I went down and after making sure that all the doors and windows were locked, I sat down and began to sew.
>
> My machine was very old and very noisy. I remember how very still the old house and town seemed whenever the machine stopped, the only sounds being the closing of the village store. One could always tell when it closed by the noise made by village loafers as they left the store. I remember thinking that soon the town would be quite deserted and I had better go upstairs. However my baby needed the dress, so I sewed on, humming a tune and thinking of how good my baby would look in his new dress. When I finished a seam and the noise of the machine stopped I heard noises that I had never

heard before; it sounded like the footsteps of several men on the kitchen porch. They stepped slow and heavy, as if they were carrying a great weight. I listened breathlessly. They made so much noise that I finally decided that it was someone trying to frighten me and made up my mind not to notice it, especially since I knew the house was locked and no one could get in.

So after listening awhile and hearing nothing, I decided to go on with my sewing. My sewing machine made so much noise that I could hear nothing else while I was using it. The seam ended. Imagine my fright when I distinctly heard the kitchen door open and the heavy steps of several men crossing the bare boards of the old kitchen and entering the dining room, directly across the hall from where I sat. I could hear them pause and then the heavy thud of a box set down on the floor. Next I heard the even tread of soldiers as they marched out of the back door. After that all was still.

Breathless and trembling with fear, I sat still awaiting I knew not what. I dared not go out in the hall to reach the stairs, for I would have to pass the door of the room in which I had heard the box set down. How long I sat there I never knew, but after a while I became more composed and I began to reason the utter impossibility of any one entering
the kitchen door, for had I not fastened it myself by placing the heavy oaken bar across it?

I made up my mind not to give way to my fears especially since I decided it must be near midnight and my husband would be home soon. I looked at the little dress.

Just one short seam to sew on the machine and then I could finish the rest by hand upstairs in my baby's room. I began to sew slowly. Before a dozen stitches were taken, above the clatter of the machine, I heard in the room opposite loud hammering, as though someone was making frantic efforts to open a heavy box. This was followed by the ripping and creaking of boards being torn from their place and of the peculiar sound made by nails and boards parting reluctantly.

I was now thoroughly frightened. I could not move and was fast losing consciousness, when above the splitting of boards, I heard my baby's shrill cry in the room above! So grasping the lamp in my trembling hand and leaving the unfinished dress fast in the machine, I opened the hall door and started for the stairs. The dining room door was closed as I passed it I could hear the frantic efforts of some one trying to open a strong box. I fled up the stairs and reached my room. As I locked and bolted my door and sank upon the bed beside my baby, a woman's scream, so shrill, so full of agony, rang through the house from the room below that my heart stood still with terror. It finally died away with moans and sobs that echoed throughout the old house. They became fainter and fainter and finally were followed by an awful silence. I distinctly remember, even in my fear, feeling acute pity for the one who was in such distress, and for days and weeks that agonizing scream rang in my ears...

The woman realized as she sat listening to Breese telling the tale that the incident she had witnessed twenty-five years earlier, one January night in 1877, had happened upon the one hundredth anniversary of the night Phyllis went mad. The explanation for the event she had lived through was so tragic that she told a reporter.

Through the years many other people have reported ghostly phenomena in the house on or around the probable date of the hanging which would have been February 22, 1777. However, the date is not exact as no written record has survived to verify the account. It is most probable that the incident happened sometime within the period from mid-January until the end of February, and this woman's account of the re-enactment in January certainly fell within that time frame.

The name of the town was changed from Vealtown to Bernardsville through the years and the Vealtown tavern was purchased by the board of trustees of the Bernardsville Public Library and was turned into the local library. The building came to local notice at that time and the woman came forward to talk to the *Newark Sunday News* about her experiences in the house at that time. This story would be the genesis of all the haunting phenomena. Until the above story was published, there were only vague rumors from local folks to indicate something occurred in the house.

Attempts to verify this account of the haunting locally have all failed. The historic records do show that a Captain John Parker did live in the area and did own Vealtown Tavern. However, no written record exists of a wife or any children including Phyllis. Captain Parker's tombstone can be found in the Basking Ridge Presbyterian Cemetery and his name is listed in the church records. There is one final discrepancy with the story. Captain Parker's date of birth has been variously listed as 1747 or 1748. This means that he would have had to have married at the age of 14 and that at the time of this event Phyllis could have been no more than 15 or 16 years old. This is not impossible, however, it does cause one to pause.

Despite the historically sketchy information there are those who will always believe that Phyllis did exist and still haunts her former home. Stories of sightings of Phyllis continue until this day.

In 1974 a seventeen year old girl named Wendy Wright approached the library where she volunteered. The doors of the building were locked upon her arrival but she peered through the windows and saw a woman with dark hair, leafing through books. Wendy thought that this woman was Geraldine Burden, the library director and she went to the front door to knock and get Ms. Burden's attention.

Despite Wendy's knocking no one came to the door. Wendy went back around to the window where she had seen the woman and looked in again. The woman was still sitting there looking through books and appeared to have been there a long time.

Once more Wendy went around to the front and as she made her away around the building she met Ms. Burden coming through the parking lot. Wendy was a bit surprised and told Ms. Burden that she had thought she was the woman in the library.

Ms. Burden was not surprised or alarmed to find that someone else was inside. It was likely that one of the other staff with keys had already arrived and was engrossed in work. The woman opened the library and Wendy followed her inside. They were quite surprised, however, when no one could be found in the building despite a thorough search.

Later on something about Wendy's sighting began bothering her. Finally the girl remembered exactly what had been wrong. She had seen the woman sitting in the hallway sitting upon a backless bench and that would not make sense. No one ever sat there to work for it was drafty and uncomfortable.

Furthermore, Wendy had seen the woman from the parking lot side of the building and that was impossible. The library had been remodeled to form the many rooms they needed and there were now walls and doors between the parking lot window and the hallway. Somehow Wendy had glimpsed a woman sitting in the building as it had looked prior to the library being placed there, but how could that be?

There was one final piece of information which only later would Wendy know was important. The sighting took place early on a dark evening on January 29, 1974. The January date would become significant when Wendy later learned the full story of Phyllis Parker. Until that time, Wendy, like so many other folks in the town, had heard that the library was haunted but they did not believe it and they never took the time to learn more about the haunting and the woman who haunted it. Wendy would learn more after that night.

In November of 1976 a group of college students from Morris County College visited the library overnight in search of Phyllis. They had toured the library with psychic investigators Ed and Lorraine Warren. Lorraine Warren claims to be psychic and she singled out a spot near the fireplace between two chairs in the Post Room as a haunted spot. She also said that she thought this place might have once been a porch or shed and that the phenomena she felt might have taken place there. Mrs. Warren was sure that the room was not there originally and she was right. That room was added by the library in 1903.

Mrs. Warren claimed to sense a male presence before the fireplace which she later identified as a doctor's. She felt that he was part of another time and that he had come back to be reunited with someone he had left behind.

In the area of the front desk she identified a grieving female spirit and she described a group of men pouring over maps and working on battle strategy while in trance. Mrs. Warren said that these men played a part in the injustice done to the doctor and the young woman and that they were not spirits but only an image from a previous time.

Mrs. Warren told the library staff that the male presence did not haunt the library but that the woman remained tied to the building because of her great grief.

The students who were part of the Unexplained Phenomenon Club of Morris County College, spent the night in the library but there were no definitive experiences to report.

Through the years others have stayed in the library over night, but aside from disquieting feelings which they admit could have been nerves, no one has ever seen or heard Phyllis.

From time to time, however, someone unexpectedly does have an unexplained experience. Martha Hammill who worked for the library during the late 1970's and early 1980's once claimed to hear indistinct voices while working alone in the library . She looked for the source of the noise and checked to be sure that the library was locked and she was alone. She found the doors still locked and there was no one else in the building, yet when she returned to the kitchen area where she was working the voices again could be heard.

Martha was unnerved about the voices and once more tried to pinpoint where they came from. She began to think they were coming from the basement door in the kitchen. She was well acquainted with the basement and decided to leave rather than go down the basement steps. She had been in the basement before and it was an uncomfortable place for her. Something frightening seemed to be there. Martha simply left the building.

On January 29th, 1987 local amateur paranormal investigator Norman Gauthier who runs the Society for Psychic Research in Manchester New Hampshire spent the night in the library along with Martha Hammill and four local reporters. This event was timed to coincide with the 210th anniversary of the original event that caused the haunting.

The reporter for the *Bernardsville News* named Sandy Stuart later wrote about the night. She described herself as "an open-minded skeptic, a non-believer who could be convinced if the right evidence presents itself."

Mr. Gauthier explained that he was not psychic and that he wanted to employ a technique known as EVP or electronic voice phenomena. This basically meant inviting any spirit in the neighborhood to imprint a message upon a tape. A new tape was placed in a recorder and the machine is turned on. People sit quietly and wait. Later when the tape is played back they hope to hear sounds, voices and messages that they did not hear when they waited while the tape ran.

Ms. Stuart, in her article which appeared in the newspaper on February 5, 1987 stated the tapes used by Mr. Gauthier were brought by a reporter in order to avoid the chance that he had pre-recorded noises to impress them. The room chosen for the taping sessions was the library reading room which was once the dining room of the Vealtown Tavern. This was the room where Dr. Wilde was brought that cold night so long ago, and this was the room where poor Phyllis wrestled the boards from the casket and went mad. It was certainly the appropriate place to try and hear ghostly sounds.

She wrote that the evening grew boring as they quietly sat about listening for any noise which could be caught on tape. If any outside noise interfered or if anyone in the room made a noise, Mr. Gauthier noted it so that it would not be mistaken later on for a significant sound.

The first session of the night was a bust. Not a single questionable sound was recorded, however, after the second session Mr. Gauthier was excited as he listened to the tape with headphones. He questioned the group and they all agreed that there were no sounds of notes that happened during the recording.

Ms. Stuart writes:

> One by one, we listen to the tape. The playback reveals some loud sounds, similar to a door opening and closing or furniture being moved. We all agree on one thing. The sounds were nothing we had noticed during the recording session.

The vigil continued and several more sessions of taping were done. Nothing further appeared until the sixth taping session. Mr. Gauthier insisted that the sounds upon the tape were "messages from the spiritual world," but it sounded like paper rattling to the reporters. They could not explain the sounds but they were not convinced either.

After the seventh taping session they heard "tavern noises" followed by footsteps and a door closing. The others agreed that the noises were unexplainable.

By 3:51 a.m. the group had entered its ninth recording session of the night. Everyone is tired but Mr. Gauthier believed he heard a man saying the word "please" on the tape. The others heard a man saying something but they could not make it out.

Ms. Stuart ended her night by writing:

> To be honest, I don't know what to believe. I definitely heard noises on tape that I did not hear in the room. And I think I felt some sort of spiritual presence.
>
> But I still wouldn't swear to the existence of ghosts.
>
> The only thing I'm sure of is that next time I'm in the library's reading room at night I'll listen very carefully to the sounds around me. And I may discreetly bring along a small tape recorder.

Reporter John Butterfield of the *Plainfield Courier-News* also was present that night and he wrote:

> Without putting too fine a point on it, something happened Thursday night during an overnight stay at the supposedly haunted borough library....
>
> ...whatever the source of the sounds heard in the early morning hours, all those present agreed that on two occasions, noises that had not been audible while the machine was recording were heard during the playback of a reel-to-reel tape. The tape they were using was a new sealed one provided by one of the reporters to eliminate the possibility of tampering.

The library has a copy of the cassette of the sounds recorded that night which patrons can listen to. Through the years many folks have also heard the sounds and to date no one has ever figured out just what "earthly" source there could have been for the noises.

On December 5, 1989 a library patron and her two sons, one approximately five years old and another son nearly four, had an encounter with Phyllis. After the Story Hour on that day, a female patron with her two sons and infant daughter was preparing to check out some books. The eldest boy wanted to go outside by himself and he ran into the front hall. His younger brother followed but the boys hesitated there as their mother forbid them to go further and kept calling to them to come back.

Children's librarian, Joanne Tuffnell witnessed the account and later wrote:

> She (the young mother) kept trying to make him (the younger boy) return to her at the desk, but he stood at the Reading Room, (the former dining room) insisting that she come. She finally did go over to him, and he said, 'Somebody's in here.' they both stepped up into the Reading Room. She looked around and saw no one.
>
> 'There it is!' he said, pointing to the center of the two fireplaces. 'There!' the mother began to wonder, looking

around again and seeing nobody. 'Who is it?' asked the mom. 'A wady,' said the little boy.

The older brother came to look but saw nothing. The mother saw nothing but got chills up and down her spine! She wanted to get out of there immediately. 'Did she talk to you?' asked the mother. 'No,' her son replied. 'Did you talk to her?' asked the mother. 'Yes,' he said, 'I said 'Hi!'

Later that night, the mom and dad were talking about it with the boys, and the mom asked what the lady was wearing. The boy said it was a dress, but it went to the floor.

The mom says her son has never heard any ghost stories about the library, and she was quite unnerved by the whole thing.

Library employee Maria Mandala was interviewed in December of 1989 for a brief article for NBC's show "Inside Edition." Maria began working in the library in 1983 and stayed there for about six and a half years. During that time Maria worked the evening shift at the library which began at 7 p.m. She usually arrived early to get things ready and she said that some evenings she heard a woman softly singing or humming though no one else was in the building. Ms. Mandala thought the music might be coming from a radio outside but found no one when she searched. She was impressed by the fact that the music was not a type popular with teens.

Maria also heard the voices which Martha Hamill had heard years before. The muttering voices did not upset Ms. Mandala but in time she came to believe that the songster was Phyllis.

Maria also told of a day when she was enjoying some coffee in the library kitchen when the telephone lights all suddenly blinked on as if there was a sudden influx of calls. The phone did not ring however, but Maria tried to answer the calls. There was no one on any of the lines, yet the lights continued to flash on all the phones as if they were awaiting an answer. This time Maria was scared and she called her husband to come over. No one ever found an explanation for the strange phone activity.

While the crew from "Inside Edition" was in town they spoke to an unlikely witness to the phenomena of Phyllis. Retired police chief John Maddaluna said that he had an experience in the building in 1950. He was then a young officer just out of the academy and had just been hired by the police force. He certainly was not concerned about ghosts at that time.

As a new officer he had to work the midnight shift with an older officer who was training him. They used flashlights to check store fronts as they walked by the various businesses, offices, and the library. As Officer Maddaluna flashed his light around the library one night, he saw a woman in a long white dress before the front room fireplace which was visible down the hall near the rear of the building. He looked through several other windows but could not see her. He again came to the front of the building and looked in once more. There was no one there!

Once more he checked the building out all around and returned to the front. Again, he shown his light inside while stepping to the side. If the person inside shot toward the light, he did not want to be in the path. Once again he saw the woman in the white dress about 20 feet away but she had not been there a few seconds earlier. In an interview that appeared in *The New York Times, October 26, 1997* Maddaluna said, "It was a nice looking girl in a white gown. I thought it was a mannequin at first, but when I put my light on it, it seemed to move. I could see her head turn a little."

Now poor Officer Maddaluna had to go back to the older officer and report his strange encounter. To his surprise the older officer did not laugh. "Don't worry about it, I have seen the same thing a couple of times," he was told. John Maddaluna would later learn that the room where he sighted the white woman was called the Post Room and it was the same room where Lorraine Warren would seventeen years later describe a "tingling" which indicated a spirit.

The library staff in the main try to downplay Phyllis and her haunting. They do not want to frighten patrons--especially children-- however they are truthful if pressed. They see Phyllis as a good spirit who should be pitied for her tragic life if she's considered at all. Phyllis is real to the staff though, and in 1988 they issued her library card number 1777. Phyllis has yet to officially use it, but why should she when she would never take the books from the building anyhow? Long before the library existed this was her home. Library employee Eileen Luz Johnston wrote a booklet entitled, *Phyllis-- The library Ghost?* in which she chronicles the history of Phyllis and her hauntings.

The stories of Phyllis continue to be reported. The Amazing Kreskin came to Bernardsville and put on a show for "Inside Edition" in August of 1992. Reporter Sandy Stuart of the *Bernardsville News* reported upon the event. Kreskin did table tipping and had tables flying about the basement where guests witnessed his show. He was reported to have said "Things happen that I can't explain... I have never seen a ghost, but I do believe there are some forces in a house that we can't explain."

During Kerskin's performance tables literally began flying about and after Kreskin spelled out Phyllis's name several people suddenly felt a terrible cold despite the rooms 80 degree temperature. One lady even claimed to have difficulty breathing. Another guest claimed that he could not control his own arm which kept rising as if someone else were pulling it up into the air. Did Kreskin reach Phyllis? He would not say. With great showmanship he left the audience wondering and wanting more.

In an article by Bev McCarron in the *Star Ledger* she says Kreskin said he believed that there was a presence in the library that night. She also noted that if Kreskin was only putting on a show, he got a bit rough. A lady was pinned to the wall by an aggressive table after Kreskin asked Phyllis Parker to give a physical sign if she was there. The table literally kept attacking this woman and she left with some bruises on her legs from the oddly aggressive table.

After the Kreskin performance in the Bernardsville library aired the library received a letter postmarked Newark, New Jersey from a gentleman who spent his childhood in Bernardsville back in 1907. The man wrote that as a child he spent many hours in the library and one summer he nearly finished reading every book in the children's section. He asked the librarian if he might take books from the adult sections and she agreed. One day as he was in the adult section he was in a stall of books looking around. He knew that he was alone in the room but suddenly he no longer felt alone. The man stepped out of the stalls and peeked around. There was no one there but he still felt a "presence" with him. Though it was disconcerting, the boy continued to look at books but he was positive that something else was in the room with him.

Through the years, he wrote, he had wondered about the incident from time to time and he even thought about writing to the library long after he moved away. However, the story of the ghost was not talked about much in 1907 and as an adult he assumed that the ghost story had long been forgotten. He decided not to write so that he would not frighten anyone--especially the librarian. Since seeing the piece on television where the Amazing Kreskin had been in the library he now felt free to share his little incident.

Unfortunately for those who like Phyllis, her days as library ghost are numbered. The Bernardsville Library has built a new building and soon Phyllis will no longer be able to wander about leafing through books. What will happen to Phyllis Parker after the people go away? Who knows? Those who believe in Phyllis hope she won't be lonely once her home is no longer the town library.

BLACK JAKE AND THE DELTA SALOON

Gambling is all about superstition and luck. Lady Luck smiles upon some and for others she turns her head in disgust. People who gamble have long had their special rituals which they believe changes their luck. Blowing on dice for good luck or genuflecting before placing a bet are only two examples. Some people have made gambling their whole life and have committed suicide because Lady Luck turned away from them. That's the story of a local gambler in Virginia City, Nevada named Black Jake.

People in the 1860's would have known exactly who you meant if you asked them about Black Jake. Jake was a colorful local figure who owned the Delta Saloon, one of the most successful saloons and gaming dens in the area. Jake, however, was addicted to his own games. He had made and lost fortunes over the gaming tables of the west before settling down to run and gamble at his own gaming den in Virginia City.

One night Jake sat down at the faro table and began to gamble. He lost hand after hand, but something seemed to drive him on that night. The debt he owed the house continued to mount and mount but Jake continued to play. The next hand would be better he thought. He knew he did not have enough money to cover the debt and he knew that there were others to answer to if he could not come up with the money. Still, Jake kept playing on.

As the night grew late, Jake continued to play. At last he had nothing left to loose. Witnesses would later say that Jake was quite calm. He simply pulled his gun from its holster by his side and put it to his head. Before anyone had time to react, Jake pulled the trigger and slumped over the faro table.

After that night that table brought only bad luck to faro players. Folks claimed to see Black Jake at the table. Many more refused to sit at the faro table because they said they saw Black Jake committing suicide repeatedly.

The table was finally removed from the Delta Saloon gaming rooms but it is still in the building. It's a display item in the casino.

People report seeing Black Jake in the building and especially at the faro table to this day. Though Jake had bad luck that night in the 1860's, his spirit seems to have brought good luck to the Delta Saloon because it's still open and still profitable. Black Jake's spirit is still at the Delta and perhaps you can see him there yourself if you're ever in the area.

> *You can call the saloon at 702-847-0788 for more information, or write to them at:*
> *Delta Saloon and Casino*
> *18 South C St.*
> *Virginia City, NV 89440*

SUNNYLAND

It should not be surprising that ghost stories and urban legends often melt together. The internet is filled with such unsubstantiated stories and Sunnyland is one of these.

In Orlando, Florida there is a large, old, abandoned hospital called Sunnyland Hospital. The building originally was a facility for treating those who had tuberculosis during the first part of the twentieth century. As advances in medicine offered vaccines to prevent tuberculosis, the hospital became a facility for the mentally insane and the mentally handicapped. There are no stories about mistreatment of the patients but many of the medical practices used upon the mentally ill during the twentieth century were forms of torture. Ice water baths, enemas, electric shock treatment, lobotomies and many other methods which seem today quite barbarous were conducted in those facilities.

In the early 1980's the facility was finally closed and the building abandoned. When the hospital shut down, they simply locked the doors leaving the beds, medical paraphernalia and, some say, the ghosts inside.

The building became a target for local vandals and today every door and window of the first two floors of the facility have been broken into. Graffiti decorates the building and some of the interior walls where the more intrepid vandals dared to go.

It must be an odd feeling to walk among moldering beds and the debris from the active days at the hospital. It would seem almost as if someone should come in at any moment or that the patients should be shambling down the halls.

There is a local mystery which has built up around the hospital. There are stories that the third floor of the old building has remained securely locked despite the vandals' best efforts to break in. What could be so securely locked in the third floor has become a matter of speculation and the more imaginative have come up with many theories.

There is no doubt, though, that for many, this building with the odd name of Sunnyland is still inhabited by something. Passersby have reported seeing shadowy figures or having heard the sounds of feet shuffling the halls in slippers. Others have told tales of hearing the cries of the patients and of hearing loud thuds as though something had fallen. The building does seem to feel ominous, but that can be attributed to the condition it is in and because of what must have occurred within it's walls. Is Sunnyland Hospital haunted? Many local folks insist that it is.

THE SOUNDS FROM HELL

Jeff Marks pulled off his shirt and tossed it on an old kitchen chair that was spilling stuffing and reached for the coffee jar to make himself a cup of lukewarm tap water coffee. Jeff caught a reflection of himself, blond and muscular, in the black glass of his kitchen window and ran a hand through his hair rumpling it. He smiled thinking of Linda, his fiancee, whom he had just left at her parents' home. He sat the cup down on the scarred surface of his kitchen table and sat down to unlace his boots and kick them off. His mind wandered back to his date with Linda as he sent the boots skittering across the pock marked linoleum. He was thinking about when he'd see her again in the morning. It wouldn't be until lunch time because she'd be going to church in the morning. Of course he could have gone with her, but he wasn't much of a church goer so he'd just wait until she and her family got back from church.

A sound caught Jeff's attention as he sat there sipping the rapidly cooling coffee. It started out low like the sound from a radio or television but it steadily increased in volume until it seemed to fill the room. A strange wailing crying sound interspersed with voices, voices that chanted something he could not quite make out. With a start he sat the cup down sloshing some coffee over the side. The voices were chanting his name. Over and over again, they called him while the pained wails flooded over, masking the chant from time to time.

Jeff's mind did some split second thinking. An explanation, he needed to figure out what was going on. He thought of each explanation, television, radio, a prank, but none sounded right. Finally he settled for a radio, though. He thought of the old radio he had in the bathroom. Maybe he'd left it turned on and a weak channel was coming in now that it was getting late. The wailing could be static or other channels interfering. Now that he had supplied a cause of the sound, he jumped up and ran to the bathroom. The sound was not as loud in there, and the radio sat mutely on a shelf not only off, but also unplugged.

Panic gripped him and Jeff had to fight off the urge to run. He stepped hesitantly back into the kitchen. The chanting took on a different tone now. The voices grew clearer. Their words made him freeze.

"Jeff! Jeff! You are ours. You are ours!"

The voices were gleefully shouting now and the sound petrified him. The wailing turned into a scream and Jeff bolted for the door, slamming it as he left. He dug in the pocket of his jeans for his keys and jumped into his car. The engine started on the first try and he slammed his bare foot against the gas pedal leaving a trail of rubber behind.

In the darkness he simply drove around feeling slightly foolish but not willing to hear the voices if they came again. He made several trips around the alley but there was no one there.

Finally Jeff found himself outside Linda's parents' home. It was nearly two o'clock by his watch but he didn't have anywhere else to go, so he dug an old pair of sneakers from the back of his car and pulled on his denim jacket against the early morning cold, and walked up the driveway to the Sheerer house.

The house was dark and Jeff felt strange as he walked up to the silent house. How was he going to explain to the Sheerers that he was afraid of voices coming from the walls of his apartment and that the only safe place he could think of in the middle of the night was Linda's home? Jeff took a deep breath and rang the door bell. The sound clanged through the house making him wince slightly. He pressed the button a second time to be sure that it awoke the Sheerers. First a patch of yellow light threw itself across the lawn as someone turned on an upstairs light, then sounds came from inside, distant at first but growing louder as they moved toward him.

Jeff squinted as the outside light blinked on briefly, then Mr. Sheerer cracked open the door.

"Jeff, what are you doing here at this time of night? Is something wrong?" Mr. Sheerer's voice faded away as he turned and addressed someone coming down the stairs. Jeff caught a glimpse of Mrs. Sheerer as she pulled on a robe.

Jeff knew, even as he said the words, that they sounded crazy. "I wondered if I could stay here tonight? I don't want to go back to my apartment. I'm afraid."Mrs. Sheerer's face appeared behind her husband. "Invite him in, Jake. I'll go make some coffee." Jeff followed Mr. Sheerer into the kitchen. "You want to tell us what this is all about?" Mr. Sheerer asked.

Jeff looked at Mrs. Sheerer who was spooning coffee into the percolator basket.

Linda came into the kitchen and sat down beside Jeff. "What's wrong, Jeff? What are you doing here at this time of night?"

Jeff barely noticed how pretty Linda was with her rumpled golden hair and short nightie and robe. His mind was still on the voices that had risen from his kitchen wall.

Alan, only two years younger than Jeff and Linda, sauntered in like it was a common thing for his family to be up in the wee hours of the morning talking to a frightened friend.

"Who's having a party," he quipped.

Mr. Sheerer eyed his son severely. "Jeff's about to tell us why he's here." He looked at Jeff. "Go on."

As Jeff began his story, Linda reached out and took his hand. He squeezed it gratefully. He told it all. Everything about the voices, the cries of pain, and how he knew that it was not a TV or a radio.

"Sounds like someone's playing a joke on you, Jeff old boy." Alan pushed his coffee cup back. "I wouldn't let it get you down."

Jeff pulled his jacket closer around himself. He was feeling very cold. He bit back a caustic reply to Alan's remarks. If someone had come to him with such a story, Jeff would have said the same thing, but that was before he had heard the voices wailing forth from his walls.

Mr. Sheerer growled at Alan to be quiet. "Jeff, I can't say that I don't believe you. There are more things in this world than we will ever be able to explain. God has many mysteries and many mysterious ways of dealing with us. Then again," he paused, rubbing his cheek in thought. "It could have been something else altogether."

Jeff tried hard not to let his frustration show. He knew that what he had heard was not a TV or a prank. He didn't know what would explain it, but he knew what it was not.

Linda shivered. "It all sounds creepy to me. It's like some horror story. I wouldn't blame you if you never went back to that terrible apartment."

"Well, I say that we should all go to bed if we're expecting to make church in the morning." Mrs. Sheerer reached across the table and patted Jeff's hand. "Why don't you take the extra bed in Alan's room tonight. We'll get this all worked out in the morning."

Alan looked at Jeff in mock seriousness. "You can stay there just as long as I don't start hearing voices, too. If I do then..." He made the "you're out" gesture with his fist and his thumb sticking out.

Jeff followed the family upstairs. Alan loaned him a robe and some extra blankets. Sleep was a long time in coming. Long after light snores attested to Alan's slumber, Jeff lay awake hearing phantom voices chasing through his head.

In the morning Mr. Sheerer agreed to take Linda and her mom to church while Alan accompanied Jeff back to his apartment. All of the way back to the apartment Alan kept up a steady stream of bantering remarks. Jeff tried to ignore them, but Alan's humor was wearing thin. Worse yet, he had begun to worry that there might have really been nothing to be frightened of. Was it possible that he had let his imagination get away from him?

NO! his mind whispered, and he shuddered as he remembered the sound of those voices.

They pulled into the gravel driveway beside the apartment. Jeff had to fight the feeling of fear that threatened to overwhelm him.

"You ready to go visit your spook?"

Jeff didn't dignify Alan's remark with an answer. He got out of the car, dug out his house key, and approached the building the way a soldier might approach an enemy encampment.

"You sure someone didn't slip something into your coffee last night?" Alan walked up beside Jeff as he unlocked the door.

A blast of cool air greeted them. Jeff listened before he stepped inside and Alan barged on in laughing at him.

"Everything's fine." He swung his arms out. "Unless you are hearing voices now, because I sure don't."

Jeff entered the apartment and tossed his keys down on the table. "I don't care what you say, Man, I heard voices in here last night."

Alan spied the cold cup of coffee still sitting on the table and sniffed the cup experimentally. "Just as I thought," he said in his best Sherlock Holmes manner. "Someone has put opium in your coffee."

Jeff grabbed the cup, spilling cold coffee down his wrist. "Give me that, Sherlock. Something happened here last night, and you won't convince me differently."

Alan shivered. "It's cold in here. You got an air conditioner or something?"

Jeff had been so frightened of hearing the chanting voices that he hadn't noticed that it was cool in there. No, not cool, cold, cold and damp like a room that had been shut up for a long time. The only heat in it came from the sun shining through the kitchen door like a ray of sanity in a waking nightmare.

"I don't have air conditioning; I'm lucky to afford the lights."

Alan had left Jeff standing in the kitchen alone. He had gone into the small living room\bedroom and was poking in the closet. Jeff noticed that Alan was not so humorous anymore. It was as if the atmosphere of the apartment had drained it from him.

"Nothing in there. Can we go now?"

"I have to get some clean clothes, hang on." Jeff dug in the basket of clean clothes sitting on the only chair and found jeans and shirts. He added a second outfit to the first one he had laid out. He was not afraid to admit that he did not relish sleeping alone in the apartment again. He would be ready if the Sheerers offered to let him sleep there again.

"I've got to get some things from the bathroom," Jeff said. "I can get a shower at your place."

Alan grunted something as Jeff disappeared through the narrow door into the little bathroom.

Jeff gathered up his toiletries as quickly as he could. He was beginning to feel a little silly, but not silly enough to take Alan home and come back alone.

At first Jeff thought that his ears were playing tricks on him. There was a faint humming from the common wall between the bathroom and kitchen. It came in and out, fading like a bad radio signal. He froze holding a tube of toothpaste in one hand. He opened his mouth to yell for Alan as he realized that it was the chanting coming and going in the wall, calling his name once more, but Alan was already yelling.

"Jeff!"

Jeff dropped the toothpaste and ran back into the kitchen. In there the sound was clearer. Chanting came and went in the wall calling his name once more. A moaning and hissing sound was in the background.

"You will come with us. We will get you. You belong to us. You will come with us, we will have you... you belong to us. You will come with us. Jeff, Jeff, you are ours. You will come with us. Jeff! You will come with..."

Jeff bolted for the door in an eerie re-in-enactment of last night. Alan followed, his blue eyes as big as saucers as they ran for the car, leaving the door open.

"Did you hear it?" he shouted. "Did you hear it?"

Jeff shook his head. "That's it! That's what I heard last night." He shuddered. There was a cold shiver playing across his spine, and he could feel goose flesh that the sun could not soothe.

"That's evil, Man!" Alan was staring in horrified fascination at the kitchen door. It was as though he were frightened that whatever they had heard would be following them.

"I ain't going back in there, ever," Jeff whispered more to himself than to Alan.

Alan looked at him for a second before going back to his vigil of the kitchen door. "Nobody asked you to. Let's just go home."

Jeff felt in his pocket for his keys, but they weren't there. With a sickening feeling he realized that not only had he left his clothes behind, but he had tossed the keys onto the kitchen table when he had grabbed the coffee cup from Alan.

"They're in the house."

"I'm not going back in."

Jeff could not help thinking that Alan had finally changed his tune.

"Walk back as far as the door, Alan." Jeff knew that he should be acting more bravely, especially in front of Linda's brother, but the truth was that he didn't feel all that brave.

Alan followed Jeff to the door. The apartment was the way it had been when they had first entered it. Jeff could see his keys laying on the table. He took a deep breath and ran in grabbing them. On the way out he snapped the lock on the door.

Neither young man spoke much on the way home. They really didn't know what to say to each other. Jeff was glad, though, that someone else had heard the voices because for a little while he had begun to question his own sanity.

When they got to the Sheerer house, they saw that the family car was back in the driveway. Mr. Sheerer met them in the yard. "How'd you boys do?" He saw their faces and stopped. "You heard it again?"

"Dad, I didn't believe him, but it was awful. I was in the kitchen when it started and it was just like Jeff said." Alan's complexion had taken on the cheesy look of someone in shock.

"It was still there. I can't go back. I just can't."

Mr. Sheerer looked at the boys severely. "I had a bad feeling on the way to church that something was wrong. I just dropped the girls off and decided to come back and check on you guys."

Jeff, move your car so that I can get mine out. We're going back there and get to the bottom of this."

Jeff nodded. Alan grabbed his father's arm in a painful lock.

"No, Dad, you don't want to do it. Whatever's in that place is bad, real bad, evil."

Mr. Sheerer looked at the boys for just a second. "Move your car, Jeff. We're going back. I think that I have an idea of how to stop those voices."

Jeff moved the car and climbed into the back seat of the Sheerer vehicle reluctantly. This was the last place he wanted to be going on a sunny spring Sunday.

"What do you have in mind?" Jeff doubted that anything could stop the voices, but he respected Mr. Sheerer so he'd give his idea a try.

Mr. Sheerer picked something up off the front seat and handed it back to Jeff. A book. Jeff recognized the unmistakable form of a leather bound Bible.

"You think that it will help?" Jeff was getting excited about Mr. Sheerer's idea. He wasn't a church goer himself, but he had grown up in a Christian family and he had heard stories of preachers praying for houses to get rid of evil spirits. It just might work.

Alan had been quiet on the ride over, but as they approached the driveway he turned to address his father. "I'm not going back in there, Dad." There was a pleading, panicky look in his eyes.

Mr. Sheerer turned off the car engine and then looked at his son. "That's all right, you just wait here."

Jeff got out of the car and followed Mr. Sheerer to the door. In one hand he carried Mr. Sheerer's Bible, in the other he held the apartment key ready to unlock his nightmare.

Jeff reached out to unlock the door, but Mr. Sheerer caught his arm. "Just a minute, Jeff."

Mr. Sheerer took his Bible and thumbed it open. He found a certain passage and marked it with his finger. He closed his eyes for a few moments in prayer. Jeff felt uncomfortable watching so he lowered his eyes and tried to utter a silent prayer himself.

"Okay, Jeff, I'm ready."

Jeff pushed open the door and stepped out of the way. Mr. Sheerer went in and listened. There was no sound. He glanced back at Jeff.

"Give it a minute. I'm usually in there for a few minutes before it starts." Mr. Sheerer motioned him inside. "It may have something to do with you, Jeff. You'd better come inside."

Reluctantly Jeff stepped into a room. He felt the hair at the back of his neck bristle a primitive warning. Just then his ears caught the first sounds. A faint moaning and the sound of voices joined in chant faded in and out. They grew stronger within seconds and Jeff had to brace himself not to bolt through the door again. Every muscle in his body tensed and his mind screamed at him to run.

Mr. Sheerer flipped open the Bible and began reading. "The Lord is my shepard; I shall not want. He maketh me to lie down in green pastures; he leadeth me beside the still waters. He restoreth my soul; he..."

The voices changed, no longer calling for Jeff.

"SHUT UP!" The voices screamed.

Mr. Sheerer glanced at Jeff, then resumed his text. "He leadeth me in the paths of righteousness for his name's..."

"SHUT UP! SHUT UP! SHUT UP!"

"For his name's sake. Yea, though I walk through the valley of the shadow of death, I will fear no evil,..."

There was more wailing, as though the voices were in great pain, but they sounded angry as well.

"SHUT UP! SHUT UP! SHUT UP! WE'LL KILL YOU!"

Jeff hadn't thought that the voices could ever get louder, but the choir was painfully loud. He looked to Mr. Sheerer for a cue. He wanted to leave, to just forget this place in the worst of ways. Mr. Sheerer looked bad. He was no longer assured. Sweat stained the arm pits of his blue Sunday suit. His face was white and sweat ran in unchecked rivulets down his forehead. He looked like a man in a great struggle. Jeff thought that was it, he was going to run, but he did not. With the greatest of efforts, Mr. Sheerer resumed reading.

"For thou art with me; thy rod and thy staff they comfort me..." Mr. Sheerer was shouting, bulging veins in his neck to be heard over the clamor of the voices. "Thou preparest a table before me in the presence of mine enemies; thou..."

"WE'LL KILL YOU, KILL YOU, KILL YOU!" The voices chanted on and on. Jeff couldn't stand it. Mr. Sheerer looked like he might explode. Jeff thought that he might be having a heart attack. He grabbed at Mr. Sheerer and thrust him out the door. Within seconds he followed closing the door.

Mr. Sheerer lay in the new grass of the small yard gasping. Jeff held his head. Alan came running from the car.

"What happened?" The chanting still sounded through the closed door.

"Get a doctor," Jeff gasped.

Mr. Sheerer grabbed Alan's hand. "No! Get me to the car."

Between them the young men got him into the back seat of the car. Jeff dug the keys from Mr. Sheerer's pocket and started the car. Alan sat in the back holding his father.

By the time that they got him to the Sheerer house he was doing a lot better. His color had returned and his breathing was normal again, but he looked tired and weak.

Jeff dropped them at the house and went for Linda and Mrs. Sheerer at church.

Linda realized that Jeff was driving her family's car before it stopped, and she ran out to meet Jeff. "What's happened? Where's Dad?"

Jeff didn't want to alarm her. "He's home, I think he's okay."

Mrs. Sheerer waved good-bye to a group of friends she had been talking to, and got into the front seat. Linda hopped in the back and Jeff started off.

At the first stop light Mrs. Sheerer dug an envelope out of her pocket book. "Here, Jeff, I nearly forgot to give this to you."

Jeff took it and tore it open while he waited for the light to turn. Printed in block letters on a single index card were the words, "Demons shall come for you in a chorus of voices."

Jeff nearly dropped the card. "Where did you get this?"

Mrs. Sheerer looked at him sharply. "An old lady came up to me after church and asked me if I knew you, and if I could give this letter to you. I don't know her. Never saw her in church before, but I said that I would. What's wrong? What does it say?"

Linda had taken the card from Jeff as he started the car moving again. Now she handed it to her mother.

Mrs. Sheerer read it, then looked at Jeff. "It's about your apartment. You can't go back there, Jeff."

"We already did." He told them about what had happened that morning, holding nothing back. The Sheerers had been drawn into this because of his involvement with them and he supposed that they deserved to know everything.

That Sunday morning was the last time that Jeff or the Sheerers ever went to the apartment. Jeff stayed with them until he found a new apartment, and then he asked friends to move his belongings out for him. He married Linda and they had several children before they eventually divorced. The happenings in the apartment stayed with Jeff for the rest of his life, but he would only tell his story to those he most trusted.

Like so many of the stories I pass on, this one was told to me by someone intimately acquainted with the principles involved. In this case it was the second wife of the man whom I called "Jeff." She insisted that when her husband had confided this story he was very shaken by it.

* *The man involved did not want the real names of those involved used.*

Doug Prindle on patrol.

Phyllis Parker's home.

Library where Phyllis Parker Haunts.

Phyllis Parker's library card.

Jackie Henningser
Old Van Buren Inn

Green Room Van Buren Inn

Van Buren Inn hall where muddy footsteps appeared.

Van Buren Inn window where woman looks out.

Van Buren Inn

The Mansions

Eastland

Recuers taking bodies from the Eastland.

Eastland rising.

Photos provided by Eastland Memorial Society.

WHAT HAUNTS THE MANSIONS HOTEL?

In the 1800's men of wealth were often self-made. They were adventurers who took risks and lived life large. Richard Craig Chambers was a man of his times. He grew up poor but he had a dream which drove him on. Chambers dreamt of striking it rich but he was not an impractical man. He looked around him and became convinced that there were fortunes to be made in the west and the best place to make such a fortune was in San Francisco.

In 1849 Richard Chambers set about making his fortune. He left his home in Richmond County, Ohio at the age of eighteen with his dream and an unshakable belief that he would succeed. On foot or horse back or any way he could, he managed to reach Sacramento just as gold fever struck the state. Chambers felt the urge, too, and began working along the American River at a place called Morman Island. After working the American River, Richard Chambers worked his way to Nevada.

Richard Chambers was a young man with a hunger that was not easy to quench. He ranged throughout the western United States looking for gold, good luck, and his future. Finally he took a job as superintendent of the Webster and Bully Boy mines owned by Senator George Hearst. Chambers had found his niche in the Utah territory, or so it seemed. He enjoyed the work and it seemed that fortune's favor fell upon him. In 1871 a rich vein of silver was found in one of the mines and this discovery would change Richard Chambers life.

Richard Chambers was a man who knew an opportunity and he quickly set about raising the capital necessary to develop the silver mine. He convinced an influential and wealthy group of men to invest in the mine, and he began work on getting the mine for himself. Eventually Richard Chambers mine superintendent, became Richard Chambers part owner as well. He called his mine the Ontario, but the locals called it "Plumas Asylum." Richard Chambers had begun to fulfill his dreams.

Richard Chambers knew that money made money and he turned his attentions to his many other interests. He wanted power and respect and those he gained by becoming one of the most important political figures in the entire western half of the United States.

Richard Chambers was a man of diversity and among his interests was that of publishing. He purchased a large newspaper which helped him gain name recognition and gave him respect with the intellectual crowd. But there was still something missing from Chambers dream for he had never forgotten his plan for fame and fortune in San Francisco.

Richard and his wife moved to San Francisco where he began construction in 1887 of what would be his dream home on ground he had purchased in Pacific Heights. Chambers built his mansion in the classic revival style. Here he entertained the most prominent citizens of San Francisco and the nation.

It might sound like Richard Chambers and his wife led charmed lives but that was not always so. He had many setbacks throughout the years and there were dreams of his he would never realize. Richard never forgot his humble roots nor how hard it had been for him as a young man, and he often gave work to people no one else would help.

Richard and his wife never were able to have any children. It is impossible to say just how painful this was for the couple, but in a time when all of those around them were talking of their families, it must have been difficult to admit that they had no children of their own. Perhaps in part to fill that void in their lives, the Chambers doted upon their two nieces. The one girl was named Claudia but the name of the other girl is no longer known.

Richard and his wife enjoyed spending time with both Claudia and her sister, and when the couple died they left their home and fortune to the girls.

Exactly why the girls decided that they could not share the huge mansion has never been known, but they had the main house moved to the eastern side of the lot and had an addition built on with a separate entrance and address. The new house was called the Hermitage. Many folks have speculated throughout the years that the decision to separate and build a second mansion was made because of Claudia Chambers' bizarre hobby. The young woman was literally mad about pigs. She collected and raised the beasts as pets.

Claudia and her sister lived for some time happily in their respective houses, but then tragedy struck Claudia. She was killed in an accident. The story has always circulated that it was a bizarre accident in which Claudia was literally cut in half.

After Claudia's death the houses were rented out but there were few people who stayed there long. The original mansion house soon gained a reputation for being haunted. People began to avoid the beautiful house, and it began to fall into disrepair. Through the years it became many things including a brothel, a flop house for the poor, and its future seemed certain. Richard Chambers mansion would soon be nothing but another derelict relic of the golden age in San Francisco, but then the mansions found a savior.

That savior was Richard Pritikin. Richard or Bob as he's often called, was charmed by the stately old mansion which he bought as a real estate venture. He could see the mansions for what he could once again make them, and not for what they had become. He purchased the place in 1977 and began restoring it. Because of Pritikin's loving care the Mansions is now a first class hotel and restaurant. Pritikin restored the houses to their Victorian splendor. The rooms, are filled with classic antiques, crystal, paintings, brocade, velvet and a pig museum. Pritikin was a New York ad executive who fell in love with the Mansions Hotel which had started out only as a business deal.

Richard Pritikin insists that he was a skeptic when he purchased the Mansions, but he quickly began hearing stories. He could not believe that all around him were crazy people hallucinating, and he soon became convinced that something was haunting his hotel. And if that something was Claudia Chambers he did not want to upset her, so he began collecting pigs of every description from stuffed to ceramic to please Claudia.

Through the past twenty-three years Richard Pritikin has amassed a collection of a different kind as well. On display in glass cases are letters from customers who have met the ghosts which haunt the Mansions along with items and photographs pertaining to the haunting. There are affidavits from people who have seen the ghosts and transcripts of seances. The collection keeps growing and so do the many stories of the ghosts of the Mansions.

Several prominent psychics have visited the Mansions through the years and they have all come away convinced of the legitimacy of the hauntings there. Among them were Ed and Lorraine Warren, parapsychologists and demonologists, who confirmed that there is a ghost in the original mansion house. However they did not feel that this spirit was harmful. They did warn Pritikin, however, that his nightly magic shows in the Mansions library were "exacerbating" the problem. They felt that Pritikin's magic routines celebrated ghosts.

Among Richard Pritikin's many accomplishments are his two books, his claim that he's the United States foremost sawist (he plays music on a saw), and he is also a magician. Each night before dinner Richard Pritikin dons his first costume and steps onto the tiny stage where he performs magic tricks and music. Wine glasses appear and birds materialize from nowhere. But nothing prepares the diners for Pritikin's best trick. He materializes a floating woman's head which is to be the likeness of Claudia Chambers.

Perhaps the most eminent psychic to ever visit the Mansions is Sylvia Brown. In 1991 Ms. Brown was invited to visit and while in a trance she revealed that there is more than one ghost haunting this lovely hotel.

"There is a girl that dresses in a turn-of-the-century maid's uniform. Sometimes people feel her presence. It's like brushing against cobwebs. She is earthbound. Her name is Rachel. She has remained fixed at nineteen. Rachel doesn't understand why people are invading her world. She feels very proprietary about the house. She had a traumatic death, had planned to marry but her life was cut short by tuberculosis. She died in a lower room, below the house."

Among the other things Ms. Brown revealed was that the Mansions had once been a brothel and later on was a type of "hospice... where people were cared for." (Quotes as transcribed by author Antoinette May.)

During this same seance an apparition appeared and was photographed. This photograph now hangs in the cases along with other memorabilia of the many hauntings.

Sylvia Brown also revealed during her trance, "There were many people who passed away..." She believes that there are several spirits in the Mansions.

In July 1992 a scientific study of the hauntings was made when the Office of Paranormal Investigation of JFK University came to the Mansions. They discovered that there were powerful electromagnetic energy forces, but only in the old half of the hotel. This is significant for two reasons. First, electromagnetic energy is associated with the haunting phenomena. And secondly, the haunting only happens in the old portion of the hotel.

There have been many people who have held seances at the hotel and during some of them there were dramatic events. Perhaps the most dramatic event happened in 1992 in the Empress Josephine Suite during a session with the ouija board. The participants were asking personal questions to help determine who and how many spirits were there. Suddenly the spirits grew greatly agitated. The ouija board went wild. Two wine glasses went flying across the room approximately fifteen feet before shattering. The glasses melted into molten lumps of glass. These glasses are now in the cases in the haunted gallery.

Author Antoinette May reported in her book, HAUNTED HOUSES OF CALIFORNIA, that during an evening she spent in the Empress Josephine Room with some friends the ouija board suddenly went crazy. It moved rapidly without any control. The entity speaking called itself "Julia." This entity was worried about her son, Henry Ross, who committed suicide in the house at the age of twenty-one. Julia asked Antoinette May and the others to help her son.

Guests have experienced hauntings throughout the older half of the hotel for many years. People report seeing a woman materialize and stand at the head of the main staircase. This apparition is said to be Claudia Chambers.

Actor Vincent Schiavelli, (who appeared briefly in the movie GHOST) claimed to see a female spirit while staying in the hotel.

Among the other guests who have encountered the ghosts were Steven M. Berez and his girlfriend. The couple felt so strongly about their experience that they wrote Mr. Pritikin a letter which he shared with me.

"Dear Mr. Pritikin,

ON THE WEEKEND OF MARCH 1ST & 2ND, 1997, MY GIRLFRIEND AND I STAYED AT YOUR HOTEL. WE CHECKED IN TO THE WONDERFUL "PRESIDENTIAL SUITE" AT APPROXIMATELY 1 PM ON SATURDAY MARCH 1ST.

WE STAYED IN THE ROOM UNTIL WE LEFT FOR DINNER AT 5 P.M. WE RETURNED TO THE ROOM AROUND 10 PM AND WERE INTERESTED IN ENJOYING THE ROOM AS WE WOULD CHECK OUT AND INTO A DIFFERENT ROOM FOR SUNDAY NIGHT'S STAY.

AT AROUND MIDNIGHT, THE WINDOW BETWEEN THE BED AND THE BATHROOM SIDE OF THE ROOM BEGAN TO BANG LOUDLY. I GOT OUT OF BED TO CHECK OUT THE CAUSE. SOMETHING WAS PUSHING THE WINDOW FROM THE INSIDE. I STUFFED A WASH TOWEL IN THE JAM WHICH CAUSED THE BANGING NOISE TO STOP. BUT, SOMETHING WAS CONTINUING TO PUSH THE WINDOW. I WALKED OVER TO THE WINDOW ONCE AGAIN AND IT STOPPED. WE BOTH WENT BACK TO SLEEP UNTIL WE WERE WOKEN AGAIN AT 1:45 AM. NOW, THE DOOR FROM THE BEDROOM TO THE HALLWAY WAS SWINGING OUT AND IN AGAIN IN RAPID HELTER SKELTER MOVEMENTS AS A WOMAN'S VOICE WAS SIGHING QUITE LOUDLY. THE ROOM WAS VERY COLD AND I WANTED TO TURN ON THE HEATER BUT WAS QUITE CONFUSED AT WHAT WE WERE BOTH WITNESSING. I DECIDED TO GET OUT OF BED AND WALK OVER TO THE HEATER BY THE DOOR. AS SOON AS I GOT OUT OF BED, THE DOOR SWUNG OUT ALL THE WAY AND STOPPED SWINGING AND THE SIGHING STOPPED AS WELL. BEFORE I COULD GET HALF WAY FROM THE BED TO THE HEATER, A CHILLING WIND BIT ME IN THE CHEST AND CHILLED ME TO THE BONE. I TURNED ON THE HEATER AND PEEKED OUT THE DOOR DOWN THE HALLWAY WHICH LEADS TO THE MAIN ROOM WITH THE BOOKSHELVES. I WAS QUITE SHOCKED TO SEE BOTH CHANDELIERS SWAYING IN OPPOSITE DIRECTIONS.

WE WERE QUITE OBVIOUSLY BEING ENTERTAINED BY A LEGITIMATE HAUNTING. I MUST SAY THAT GHOSTS WERE SOMETHING I HAVE THOUGHT ABOUT WITH MUCH SKEPTICISM. BUT, AS OF THAT NIGHT, I TAKE THE SUBJECT MUCH MORE SERIOUSLY.

MY GIRLFRIEND IS A PHOTOGRAPHER AND WISHED TO TAKE SOME PICTURES OF THE ROOM AND US BEFORE WE CHECKED OUT. SHE HAD ME LEAN AGAINST ONE OF THE BOOKSHELVES ONLY TO DISCOVER THAT HER HIGH QUALITY 35 MM CAMERA WOULD NOT FUNCTION. WE TOOK THE CAMERA TO THE REPAIR SHOP ON MONDAY, MARCH 3, 1997. WE WERE QUITE SURPRISED TO LEARN THAT THE CAMERA WAS FUNCTIONING FINE. THERE WAS ABSOLUTELY NOTHING WRONG WITH IT. BUT, I CAN ASSURE YOU THAT IT PLAIN AND SIMPLY WOULD NOT FUNCTION SUNDAY MORNING IN THAT ROOM.

ALTHOUGH DISTURBING, THIS WAS ONE OF THE MOST INCREDIBLE STAYS I HAVE EVER EXPERIENCED. WE BOTH HAVE NOT STOPPED TALKING ABOUT IT SINCE AND MOST LIKELY NEVER WILL.

VERY TRULY YOURS,

STEVEN M. BEREZ"

Another guest had a similar encounter in the Presidential Suite on March 8th, 1997, but this one upset her so much that she requested a room change. She wrote to Mr. Pritikin:

"...as I checked the room there were areas with dramatic temperature changes, so I proceeded to close the windows. One closed fine, two were extremely hard to close, the one opened three times, the last time I jammed it shut...I tried to switch the lights off, over and over. Only one light stayed off, both chandeliers remained on."

The next night this same customer had another experience. "...Everyone went to sleep except myself. The guests next door were talking, when at about 1:00 AM the bed started moving up and down. It was hard to believe as the head board is actually bolted to the wall. I put my book down I was reading and sat up. About 5 to 10 minutes later it did it again... I prayed over all of them (her family members) and finally dozed off."

March 11th, 1997
"...I went downstairs to the front desk and told Dean (the clerk) I was not having my girls in that room again...He agreed to move us."
Yet another couple, Mr. and Mrs. Hessig, in the Presidential Suite had such an unusual experience on June 25, 1996 that he wrote to Mr. Pritikin about it.

"...My wife had moved the stuffed pig (a musical part of the pig museum collection) from the bed to a chair across the room shortly after we arrived. Several hours later she sat on the bed to call our 5 year-old daughter, Ali. The moment Ali picked up the phone the pig burst forth with an oinking rendition of "Jingle Bells." No one had touched that pig in hours. About an hour later I was sitting in the living room when I heard the squeaky bedroom door being opened and closed repeatedly. I went to see why my wife was doing this. As I entered the bedroom I didn't see her. She had been in the shower for the last fifteen minutes...."

Guests have reported cold spots, shadows that moved by themselves, ghostly entities, noises such as foot steps and sighs, and even a toilet seat that flew across the room. There seems to be no end to the phenomena at the Mansions.

The Mansions is a first class hotel and restaurant where people like John Kennedy Jr., Robin Williams and Barbara Streisand have visited. Ms. Streisand spent a night in the Empress Josephine Suite. (No word on if she saw the ghost.)

A stay at the Mansions is well worth the investment. Located near Fisherman's Wharf, Union Square, and some of the best shopping in the city, it is an ideal vacation spot. The service, the floor shows, and the food will impress any guest. And if you don't fancy a ghost in your room, simply tell the clerk when making reservations and you will be accommodated in the new section of the hotel where no hauntings occur. You can expect a little surprise gift, a complete breakfast, a magic museum, tons of great historical artifacts to look at, a Reading Room, and much more when staying at the Mansions. Oh, and if you do happen to meet Claudia or one of her fellow haunts, don't forget to tell Richard Pritikin and me. We'll be most anxious to hear of your visitor.

THE HOBO

The sound of snow clicking against the window panes made Millie Cramer a bit sad. It was snowing hard but the forecasters were saying that the West Virginia area where she lived would soon be out of the storm. Millie hoped so. There had to be at least two feet of snow outside already, and she dreaded the thought of having to go out in the morning and shovel it. At her age shoveling snow was a bit of a job.

Millie puttered around her kitchen making a light supper and took it into the living room to eat while she watched television. Perhaps she missed her husband more at supper time than at any other time of day--except bedtime. They had been married for thirty-two years before he had gotten sick. It still amazed her to think of how quickly the cancer had raged through his body. He had been dead only nine months after it was diagnosed and he had been dead for only three months now.

Millie sighed as she sat down with her sandwich and tried to concentrate upon the flickering images on the screen. She picked at the sandwich, then laid it back down. She had always been a small woman and had never been a big eater but now she knew that she was seriously jeopardizing her health because of her bad eating habits. Sometimes days would go by before she'd eat anything more than coffee and toast. Food, like everything else in life, just was not the same since Jake had died.

Even Millie's faith had been affected by Jake's passing. She had never really questioned God, taking him for granted. She had always been a good, church-going woman and had believed in God, but now she could not help wondering if she had been wrong for all those years? What if there was nothing after life? What if she wouldn't see Jake again one day? Doubts nagged at her and that made her feel guilty. She had never doubted God before.

Millie found herself praying more and more often that God would send her a sign that He was there. She had come to a crisis point in her life, and now she needed reassurance and comfort...she just needed God to reach out in some way.

The television show barely captured Millie's mind for a little while and she tried to focus more fully on it. Suddenly she heard a knock on the door. Instantly her eyes went to the clock. It was after eight p.m. Who would be out in this storm and why would they be at her door? Immediately the apprehension and dread fell on her as it always did now that Jake was not there. She had not realized how much she had come to count on him for comfort and protection in her life until he was gone.

The knocking came again and Millie got up to answer it.

She pulled aside the curtain and peeked out. A strange man in layers of ratty clothes was huddled before her door shivering. She was afraid to open the door, so she just flipped on the porch light and called out to him through the closed door. "What do you want?"

The hobo looked up, blowing on his hands to warm them, and smiled at her. "I'm sorry to bother you, Ma'am, but I really am in need. Could you spare a bit of food for me? I haven't eaten for nearly two days." There was an earnest pleading in the man's voice that made Millie believe him. Still, she had to remember not to be too trusting.

"Ma'am, I'll accept anything you can give me; it doesn't have to be much." The pleading in the roughly clad stranger's voice pricked her conscious. Never before had she ever turned anyone away from her door hungry.

"I'll get you something to eat, but you'll have to eat out there on the porch. I can't let you in." She tried to sound strong, but she knew she hadn't been.

The hobo nodded. "I understand. I'll just wait here."

Quickly Millie hurried to the kitchen and prepared the man a meal. She opened a can of soup and heated it. While the soup warmed, she made two thick lunch meat sandwiches and added a couple apples from the crisper. She made the man a large mug of steaming coffee and set the meal on a tray. Carefully she took the tray the hallway and sat it on the floor beside the door before she looked out. The hobo was still there and she tapped the door.

"You go down off the porch now and I'll slip the tray out. I'm sorry, but I don't want to take any chances." Millie knew that she had already let the man know that she was alone by her actions, but she couldn't help herself.

The hobo nodded and hurried down the steps. Quickly Millie unlocked the door and slid the tray out with her foot while she watched the man at the foot of the steps. At least it has stopped snowing and there is no wind, she thought briefly, and I didn't have to make him stand in a snow storm.

The hobo never made a move until she had safely clicked the door shut. She shot the locks into place and looked out. The hobo had the tray and was sitting on a porch chair.

Millie didn't want to embarrass the man by watching, so she tapped the door to get his attention. "You just knock to let me know when you're done," she called out before dropping the curtain back into place.

In the living room, once more, she tried to concentrate upon the show, but her mind kept going back to the hobo on her porch. He had seemed so cold. He didn't even have a proper coat and gloves.

Reluctantly she got up and went upstairs. She opened the closet door and took out her Jake's heavy winter coat and his gloves, hat and scarf. She held them up to her face and breathed in deeply of his scent. It seemed a travesty to her that his scent had lasted longer than he had. It was all she still had of him and she had meant to keep them. She hadn't given them away with the rest of the clothing her daughter had helped her pack up after Jake's death. But now, her mind kept going back to the cold man outside. It was a sin to keep Jake's things when someone had such a need for them.

Millie tried to be brave as she bundled the garments up and carried them downstairs. The man was still on the porch but she couldn't see the tray from the window. He had taken it to a small table she and Jake had enjoyed meals on during the summer months. She tapped on the door and the hobo got up and came over.

Millie held up the coat and other garments. "I'd like for you to have these," she called loudly, and was surprised by how strong her voice sounded now. "I'll leave them for you on the little back porch. You go around and get them after you eat, okay?" The hobo nodded and thanked her.

Millie hurried to the back porch and laid the bundle of clothes there. Her heart was breaking at giving up this last bit of Jake, but it was the right thing to do. Jake would not have wanted her to do anything else.

Millie sat quietly in her living room waiting for a knock on the front door to signal that the hobo was done. None came.

One hour slipped by and then another. Finally it was nearly eleven p.m. and Millie got up to see if he was still there. There was no one on the porch.

Carefully she opened the door and peered cautiously out. Nothing moved, even in the deep shadows, and she stepped out onto the porch.

Confusion set in as she turned toward the little area where the small table was. There sat the tray still filled with food which had not been touched. Beside the tray lay Jake's coat neatly draped over a chair and his other outer wear was laying on the table.

Why hadn't the hobo eaten? Why hadn't he taken the clothes when he had been so cold and hungry?

Millie walked over and picked up the coat and tray. She carried them quickly to the door and suddenly felt an urge to turn around. Something about the porch had been bothering her and now she realized what it was. The steps...there were no footprints. She walked over to the steps as if to confirm what her eyes had already told her. The snow lay in a neat layer across the steps and there were no tracks leading up the walk or through the yard. The hobo had to have come up the steps at least twice and gone down at least twice so why wasn't the snow disturbed? She clearly remembered that it had stopped snowing before the man had gone down the steps so that she could set his meal out. How could he have left no tracks?

Millie quickly hurried back into the house. She took the tray to the kitchen and suddenly stopped dead in her tracks. It was as if a voice filled her head and she knew the answer clearly.

"Be kind to strangers for you never know when you might be entertaining angels..." It was an angel. It was her sign. God had sent her an angel to let her know that he was there and Jake would be with her again one day. He had also taught her another lesson with his hobo angel and she put the tray on the table as she slipped into a chair and began to cry.

God had told her that it was time to let go of her mourning for Jake. She needed to care more about life than death. She needed to release her pain and join the living again. She would never stop hurting for Jake, how could she after thirty-five years of loving him? But by her willingness to feed the hobo and give him Jake's clothes, she had done God's will even when it hurt and he understood and loved her for it.

Millie would tell her story many times through the years. Some folks would believe her and others would laugh it off, but none of that really mattered because Millie knew what she had seen and it was proof enough for her. A hobo angel had given her back hope and the ability to care again.

The woman's name has been changed at the request of the family.

FROM BEYOND THE GRAVE

1905

Though most parents try not to play favorites, it's only human nature that sometimes one child is favored over another. An especially easy-going child is more fun than the difficult one, or a child with similar interests to a parent will often garner more attention than the one who wants nothing to do with the parents. It was like that for James Chaffin, a farmer in North Carolina. Despite his best efforts, James liked his third son, Marshall, best. He loved all four of his sons, but Marshall was somehow closer to him.

In November of 1905 James decided to make out a will leaving his farm and all of his possessions to his son Marshall. He left not a penny nor even a memento for his other sons, Abner, John, and James P., nor was there any bequest for his wife. Chaffin must have known at the time how he was slighting his other sons, but still he made that will.

James did not have a clear conscious about his will for years. In 1919, after reading the story of Jacob and Esau in Genesis Chapter 27, he began to worry about the consequence of his action. Would his will cause anger, hatred, perhaps even bloodshed? The old man could not dare risk it, so he wrote out a new will which distributed his goods to his four sons equally. Now James had peace of mind; but then James did something with his will which seemed inexplicable. He took the will and hid it in his father's Bible in Chapter 27 of Geneses. Perhaps he meant to tell someone where to find this new will, but he didn't. Instead he wrote a note saying, "Read the 27th Chapter of Genesis in my daddie's old Bible." This note he tied up with string and hid in the inner pocket of his best overcoat. He then sewed up the pocket and said nothing about it.

James Chaffin died four years later on September 7, 1921 when he took a bad fall. The family found his first will which he had never destroyed and probated it in court. No one ever dreamed that a second, newer will existed.

Marshall and his family inherited everything, though his brothers did not seem to resent him for his great fortune. They continued to talk, and even their mother did not seem to feel slighted.

James, however, was not resting easy in the afterlife. He had made a mistake to hide his new will so well and this needed rectified.

Nearly four years after the will had been probated James P. Chaffin, the son, began having dreams in which his father came to him. He said it was as if he was awake and saw his father standing quietly looking down at him. After a few weeks the dreams stopped only to return again.

This time, however, old Mr. Chaffin appeared by the bed wearing his good overcoat. He pulled open the coat to show the pocket he had sewn up. "My will is in my overcoat pocket." With those words old Mr. Chaffin was gone.

This time James P. felt that what he had seen was not a dream but more of a vision. He was deeply impressed by his father's visit.

Early on the morning after the dream or vision, James P. visited his mother and asked about his father's overcoat. She told him that she'd given the coat to his brother John. He visited his brother a few days later and inquired about the overcoat. This time, however, James had brought witnesses with him to examine the coat. If his father had desired to right some past wrong, he wanted witnesses there to prove that he was right.

John brought the overcoat to his brother who quickly found the sewn pocket. They tore open the stitching and read the note. Together with the witnesses, they went to their mother's home and asked for their grandfather's Bible. Mrs. Chaffin brought her sons the book. Quickly they turned to the 27th Chapter of Genesis and found the new will.

This new will was duly taken to court and was probated, which made the previous will invalid. Marshall Chaffin had died by this time, but he left behind one son and a wife who contested this new will.

Just before the trial was to begin, James P. had another vision of his father. This time the old man approached the bed and asked what his son had done with the old will. James seemed to believe that this was his father's way of telling him the new will would stand.

At the trial the widow Chaffin asked to read the will for herself. After she and her son read the will, they actually agreed that the will was written in her dead father-in-law's hand. The widow and her son dropped their protest and the will had no further trouble going through.

Skeptics at the time claimed that James had forged a will which fairly distributed the wealth and cooked up the story to explain it's sudden emergence. Of course, that would not explain why the entire family agreed that the will was penned in old Mr. Chaffin's hand, surely someone would have spotted a fraud.

Other explanations suggested that John P.'s subconscious forced him to remember the new will as he slept. But would he really be thinking about the will four years after it had been probated? Another popular theory was that the family attorney knew of the will but could not locate it. He then helped concoct a forgery and helped speed it through the court system.

There is one final explanation. James P. Chaffin could have been telling the whole truth. Perhaps his father's spirit could not rest knowing that three of his sons were slighted and he came to James P. for help. Can a person reach out from the grave to right an injustice? History is filled with such stories and surely they can not all be wrong.

SAN ANTONIO'S LOST CHILDREN

The death of a child.... Nothing fills us with more sorrow than the death of an innocent child. How often have we shuddered as the newscaster told us about children who died in a car collision, an accident, or a bus crash? We feel a thread of fear unlike any other. Those who have children find their minds involuntarily going toward the unthinkable. Thank God that their children are safe, but we all ache for those parents not as fortunate. In San Antonio, Texas there has long been the story of children who died in a terrible accident, but those children have made it their personal mission to save others from a similar fate.

In the early 1940's a school bus stalled one afternoon upon the railroad tracks on the South Side on a road called Mission Road. Desperately the driver tried to restart the bus, but the bus would not start. Within seconds, terror filled the bus for a train was headed straight toward them! It roared and clanked like a live beast bearing down on them. The train screamed a warning as the engineer tried to stop the train, but stopping a train takes time.

The driver realized that death was eminent, he had to get the children out, but there was no time. The bus was struck, and ten grade-school-aged children were killed in the accident. The town was devastated. Loosing so many children was almost more than the community could bear, but life does go on. The families of the children continued to mourn their dead, but the town moved on. Still, people crossing the tracks often thought briefly of those little souls lost there so very recently.

No one is sure exactly how long after the bus crash the stories began, but soon people were talking. One day a car stalled out on the track and the frantic driver tried to start the engine. The car did not start. Amazingly, the car began to creep forward inch by inch despite being at the bottom of a small hill. The driver must have been very surprised.

The driver looked up frantically, but no one could be seen in the mirrors. Whoever was pushing the car was invisible. The car was pushed off the tracks to safety, and the driver told the tale. Soon others deliberately began to stall their cars on the tracks. They put the car in neutral and waited. The cars began to ease forward up the hill. No human agency pushed them, yet they did move forward until they were safely off the tracks.

People would say they saw the hand prints of small children in the dust on the back of their cars. It was not long before the death of the children on the school bus and the strange way cars reacted upon the railroad tracks were connected. People said that the dead children were pushing the cars. They were saving other people from a death like their own.

Today testing the ghosts has become a sort of tradition and tourist attraction. Each day several people stop on the tracks, turn off the car while it's in neutral and take their foot off the brake. To their surprise the car begins to move forward and picks up a bit of speed until it's safely off the tracks and up the little hill. They usually have to brake to stop the car as it reaches the bottom of the hill.

A reporter from a television series entitled MYSTERIES, MAGIC AND MIRACLES, Susan O'Leary, visited San Antonio in the mid-1980's and tried to have her car pushed forward. To make it easier to see the finger prints she sprinkled talc powder across the back bumper of the vehicle. O'Leary then stopped the car and followed the directions she had been given. To her surprise and apparent delight, the vehicle did move forward until the car was well away from the tracks. It seemed that this local legend was true.

Of course, skeptics like to point out that there are other "wrong way" places in the world where vehicles can go up hill. These are caused by magnetic fields within the earth that seem to reverse the gravitational pull. The skeptics can't explain, though, why this was never noticed before the children died, and why the bus was not pulled to safety with the children on it. They also can't explain why no one has tried putting other metallic objects on the road to see if they are also moved.

In the television article by Susan O'Leary, she told the story of a woman named Paula Williams, who was driving through the South Side of San Antonio one night in 1984. To Williams surprise, she saw a little girl about ten years old standing alone beside the road. The child seemed lost or confused to the woman.

Paula Williams stopped and offered the girl a ride home. The child spoke little. She got into the car and gave her address. Paula made sure that the child was properly belted in and the passenger door locked before she began.

While they drove along, Paula began to feel uncomfortable. She glanced repeatedly at the child, but the little girl did not talk. Paula asked the child her name and the little girl said briefly, "Cindy Sue."

Paula noticed that the child seemed to stare right through her in a disconcerting way. They passed over a railroad track and the child's eyes fixed upon the railroad crossing sign which she stared at intently.

Finally Paula Williams pulled into the driveway at the address the child had given her. The child seemed to hesitate. It seemed to Paula that the little girl was reluctant to go inside. Perhaps the child had a difficult time at home Paula thought, and she told Cindy Sue to stay in the car. She would go to the house and smooth the way for the little girl's return.

Paula made her way to a screen door. The inside door was open and a woman came forward to answer Paula's knock. As soon as Paula began to explain the situation, the woman grew agitated and began to shout. She threatened to call the police. "Just let Cindy Sue rest in peace!" she shouted at the mystified Paula Williams.

Paula went back to her car unnerved and confused. Something about the woman's words had struck her odd. "Just let Cindy Sue rest in peace!" That sounded like something you would say about a dead person.

At the car Paula received a further shock. The passenger side door was still locked and the seat belt was still firmly in position across the seat, but the little girl was gone. Was it possible that Cindy Sue was one of the children who had died on the tracks that day so long ago, and was she now trying to find a way to go home?

There was little that Paula could do but get back into her car and start home. As she drove along, she still felt unnerved. Something about the area seemed odd to her. Paula Williams watched street sign after street sign go by, and she realized that each street was named after a child. A memorial to those lost children of the railroad tracks. Later Paula would learn the story of the ghost children of San Antonio's South Side. She would never forget little Cindy Sue who has not yet made it home.

The ghost children are not frightening, but they are pitiful. Their helpful nature and their care for others makes them truly unique in the annals of hauntings. Very few ghosts are inclined or capable of preventing a similar fate from happening to others. It is a testament to these children that love for their fellow man has kept them here watching and waiting for an opportunity to help. Since that terrible day in the 1940's when the children died, not one person has died at that railroad crossing. Somehow each time an accident seems eminent the car is mysteriously moved just in time.

If you are ever able to go to the South Side of San Antonio on Mission Road, go ahead and stop your car. Let the children push you to safety, but don't be frightened. Just whisper a small 'thank you' to the children, and say a prayer that they are happy as they keep their ever vigilant watch at the railroad track. Personally, I hope that one day the children all find a way to go home.

THE CRYING GIRL

In Aloha, Oregon there stands an old two-story frame house which is much like many houses built around the turn of the century in the Portland area. The house has a cement basement and an unfinished attic like many homes and this house is located on a two-acre lot much like many other houses on that street, but what makes this house different is that the owner, Gerald Reed raised his family there and believes that this house is haunted.

In the mid-1960's Gerald and his wife began looking for a home in the Aloha area. There were few homes that they could find which would suit them both. In fact, there were very few homes in the area for sale and still fewer that the young family could afford. Gerald's wife had wanted to settle for a "fixer-upper" but none of the homes she found seemed feasible to Gerald. The couple had been looking for a home for over a year by that time. Gerald remembered driving around with his first wife as they passed through the streets of the little town and feeling the frustration and hopelessness of the situation. "Someone's gonna have to die before we find a place around here," his wife muttered. It was a dark joke but Gerald shared her frustration and he agreed. He did not know how prophetic the joke would become.

Several more months of house hunting brought the young couple no closer to finding a home. One day a real estate agent in the Aloha area phoned the Reeds and told them that there was a house just coming on the market in the little town which might just fit their needs. It seemed that the old man who owned the place no longer wanted to live there since his wife had died. The old fellow had decided to put the house up for rent for the time being until he could decide exactly what he should do.

Gerald Reed and his wife made arrangements to go visit the house but they were not very hopeful. It was about 9:30 a.m. when they set out to see the property and it was a cold, rainy winter day. The rain at times felt like sleet and the couple had to be careful of the road conditions. Furthermore, Gerald, kept hearing the real estate agent's last words from his phone call. "The place has potential but I want to warn you now, the old place does need a lot of work."

The Reeds located the property and took a look. Neither one was impressed by it. The old house had been owned by a family in the late 1930's who had raised a family there. There were many old fruit trees dotting the property; a rose garden also remained there but hadn't been well cared for. The garage had a broken door that hung crooked. There was a chicken coop but it was in terrible shape. The roof had huge holes, the floor was missing in places and the windows had been torn out. The building was a real derelict. The other out buildings were in just as bad a shape.

The old house made Gerald want to moan. "Not again," he thought dismally as he followed the agent up to the house. It was like all the other properties they had seen. The house needed more than just work.

There was no heat in the house and the Reeds were thoroughly wet from their tour of the grounds. They shivered inside their coats as they stepped inside, but immediately Gerald felt that there was something different about this house. It radiated warmth. The couple felt at home, comfortable in the place. Despite the terrible state of the house, Gerald knew that this would be their home. If he had been pressed, he would have had difficulty explaining why this dilapidated house was different from the dozens of others he'd seen, but it was different. The Reeds knew they had found not a house but rather their home.

They rented the property and moved in. Gerald began work upon the house and enjoyed it much more than he had anticipated. Eventually they were offered an opportunity to purchase the house and they did so. This was a house which they both loved.

The Reeds lived on the first floor of the house and rented the second floor to a single mother who had two children. During this time Gerald remembered that his daughter Teri had come to him once with a story about a spirit on the second floor. Gerald was quite busy and did not pay her story much attention at the time. He was busy and happy working on the house.

Teri told her father that she and Janie (the little girl who lived on the second floor) had been in the unfinished part of the attic with flashlights, trying to scare each other when they decided to go down a little walkway through an area where there was no flooring yet. It was a dangerous place and the girls knew they shouldn't have been in the area, but the urge to explore was strong for the little six-year olds.

Teri and Janie had begun down the narrow catwalk when their attention was captured by a white goat shaped head with a skeleton body--the head had long horns like a Texas long hour might have. The figure had a flowing, white pulsing light around it. The goat's head spoke to the frightened children.

"What are you girls doing here?"

Janie pulled at Teri and they ran downstairs where they found Gerald and told him the tale. At the time Gerald had been busy but just the knowledge that the children had been in such a dangerous place had caused him to react. He hurried upstairs and looked around. He found nothing but he realized that if the little girls had not been frightened away from the catwalk they could have fallen through the ceiling below them to their deaths. As he stood there looking around, an uncomfortable feeling came over him. It was as if someone unseen was near him. He hurried back downstairs to the children and tried to persuade himself that the feeling had only been imagination.

It would be many years later that Teri would once again bring up that incident. She told the story as an adult with as much conviction as she had when she was six-years-old. Teri truly did see that odd figure and she would tell her father that she believed that the spirit had been trying to help her and Janie stay safe by scaring them away from a dangerous place.

The Reeds had been having marital problems before coming to the house and those problems continued. Eventually the Reeds split up but remained civil because of their children.

Gerald Reed rented the house out and moved back to Portland after the divorce. He was grieved, though, when he returned to Aloha and realized that the renters were abusing the house he had worked so hard on. He found other renters to move in eventually but they, too, did not take care of the place.

The third renters were different, though. They felt the same love for the house that Gerald did. He felt comfortable with these folks in the house. The renters approached him about buying the house but Gerald was not sure he wanted to sell it.

The third renters called Gerald one night, though and began a strange conversation which stirred old memories in Gerald's mind.

The renters asked, "Mr. Reed, did you have---are there any ghosts out here in the house?"

Gerald Reed was only momentarily surprised by the odd question. He had never seen any spirits while he lived there but something about this idea was familiar to him. He did not want to loose such good tenants so he was hesitant.

"What's happened?" he asked.

The renter seemed to pause as though looking for a reasonable way to explain the situation. "We hear a child crying. It's in the building. We don't know much about it. Did you ever hear it?" There was almost a hopeful tone in the renter's voice.

For a moment Gerald thought back to his daughter Teri's experience but he had never heard anything. Still, he had always had a warm, welcomed feeling in the house almost as if someone unseen had wanted the Reed family there. He opened his mouth to tell the renter that there had been no crying girl ghost there when he lived in the house, but that's not what he said.

"Oh, that one. Well, could be she's worried about you. Just tell her she's welcome to stay and she'll be quiet. She must like you." What on earth had possessed him to say such a thing! Somehow Gerald had a strong conviction that he had just told the absolute truth, though he had no reason to believe it.

Later his renters would tell him that they had spoken to the crying girl when she was heard again. They had reassured her that they were not going anywhere and that she was welcome to stay with them. After that the spirit was no longer heard crying.

Gerald Reed believes that the house in Aloha, Oregon just might be haunted and that if it is the spirit there is gentle and loving. Perhaps it is even a little girl who is looking for a loving family still.

Teri Reed is now a married woman named Teri Garza who has children of her own and she knows the house in Aloha is haunted by a spirit which tried to protect her and her friend Janie long ago from a dangerous place. When I interviewed her about the incident, she was clear and concise. Her story was exactly as her father had related it.

She and Janie had dared each other into the attic because the older boys would go there and it was a place off limits to the children. They had been about to go down the dangerous catwalk when a goat's head figure appeared at the far end against the solid wall. The figure had round eyes, a round mouth and no nostrils. It spoke and asked the children what they were doing there. Janie had pulled her away and they had run to tell Teri's father.

Teri believes that the spirit there was good and wanted to keep those who lived there from harm. Gerald believes that, too, and so he still has great love for his old home in Aloha even though he and his second wife make their home in Portland today.

Because there are people living in the house today and it is a private residence, Mr. Reed, has asked that I not give the exact location of the house. I was happy to honor his wishes. He is a very nice gentleman who still cares for the house and wanted his story told, but he did not want to bring undue publicity to those who now live in the house.

"PLAY FOR ME, BETH."

Through the years the Martha Washington Inn in Abingdon, Virginia has seen a great deal of history and no doubt that history has left an imprint upon the building. But there was one event in the history of United States which left far more than impressions upon this beautiful, historic inn, than any other. The building was built in 1832 as a manor house, but the sixty-one-room building soon found other uses. Before the Civil War the building was a women's college, but it would be the war which would forever mark this building.

The Civil War was the worst conflict this nation has ever engaged in. It was an especially emotional war. Brother against brother, neighbor against neighbor and no one ever knowing quite where to stand on the issues. It was especially hard on America and perhaps that is why there are so many spirits at the Martha Washington which date from that tragic, turbulent time.

During the Civil War the building was used as a hospital. Here unimagined horrors were seen. There were the amputations, the terrible pain, gangrene, shattered bones, and terrible stab wounds not to mention, dysentery and a multitude of other diseases that decimated the forces on both sides.

During the time that the building served as a hospital, a young woman named Beth came to work there. Beth was a nursing student and she was a brave and caring girl. Whether the soldiers were from the south or the north, she felt great compassion and took the best care of them that she could.

Beth's life was forever changed when a Confederate soldier named John Stoves came into the ward Beth worked in. Immediately she seemed to sense something special about the man and she spent whatever free time she could manage at his bedside. Today no record remains of why John had come to the hospital but he was there for several weeks.

Beth and John fell in love and it was a passionate affair of the heart. They spoke about promises that Beth was afraid would never happen. She had seen the looks that passed between the nurses and physicians as they examined John. She, too, could see that John was growing ever weaker despite her tender ministrations.

Beth occasionally would go up to the ward in the evening and play her violin for the patients. It was a relief from the terrible daily grind to hear the lovely music slowly drifting through the building.

John too, loved Beth's playing and as his illness progressed, he seemed to want her to play more and more. Beth would ask her beloved what she could do to ease him and John would grasp her hand in his feeble grip and whisper, "Play for me, Beth. Just play for me."

One day Beth came to John's side and she must have known then that his end was near. He was pale, wasted and gaunt. She leaned down to John and spoke to him softly.

"Play for me, Beth," he whispered through dry lips.

Beth began to play her violin and the music filled the ward. She watched John for a while, but he closed his eyes and she tried to tell herself that he was only resting though her treacherous mind told her the truth. John had slipped away from her while she had comforted him in the only way left to her.

Beth was inconsolable after John's death. She stumbled about her work and seemed to have lost her own will to survive. Within weeks Beth became ill and died. After that people began to see her spirit throughout the building, but she seems to linger in the room where John Stove passed away. Perhaps she is waiting for him to come collect her or perhaps in her grief she never realized that John must be waiting for her on the other side.

Of course, there are other ghosts from the Civil War also attached to the inn. On the south lawn of the inn a horse has been seen from time to time on dark nights. The horse is just milling around as if waiting for someone to come collect it. However, if anyone tries to approach it, they find no horse there. The story of the man the horse is eternally waiting for is a sad one.

In 1864 a group of Union soldiers were ambushed by Confederate raiders near the tavern. One of the Union soldiers was wounded and his comrades carried him into the nearby inn for help. At that time the building was already a hospital and there they found assistance, but it was too late. Around midnight the Union soldier died.

When the Union soldiers had taken their buddy into the hospital, they had let his horse wander free. All night no one gave a thought to the poor beast waiting for it's now dead master. In the morning they remembered the beast but no one could find it. It was never seen again. What happened to the horse would never be known, but when a ghostly horse began appearing upon the south lawn people associated it with the dead Union soldier and believed that the beast had eventually died only to return to where it had last seen it's master.

> *If you want to visit the Martha Washington Inn, phone 1-800-533-1014 for reservations.*

THE HAUNTINGS AT BERLIN'S OLD PALACE

In Berlin, Germany a building long known as the Old Palace once instilled fear and awe. The building was built in 1699 by the wild Frederick Hohenzollerns, the first King of Prussia. King Frederick was determined that his palace would be the envy of all Europe, and when he was done he was right. The building was a large, grand affair with six hundred rooms, large courts teaming with people and an opulence which has rarely been equaled. King Frederick was absolute ruler and none stood between him and his own ideas. He could put to death an innocent man as quickly as a guilty one. All of his subjects lived in fear of him.

One of the most feared parts of the palace was the Tower of the Green Hat. This was the interrogation room. Here many devices of torture were housed and the mistress of this area was the Iron Maiden. This archaic device was used to elicit confessions from those who dared to not bow to King Frederick's will. Unfortunately, after a stint in the Iron Maiden a confession was really a moot point.

The palace, though, had many other chambers including some of the finest bedrooms in all of Europe. The rooms were decorated with the most expensive and impressive antiques King Frederick found and were known for being breathtakingly lovely. Unfortunately, though, the chambers like the Tower of the Green Hat gave this lovely palace a sinister air. It was little wonder that people whispered of ghosts when they entered the halls of this palace.

For hundreds of years the palace stood as a royal building, but in 1914 the world changed with the advent of World War I. The palace became only another office building, still the stories of the haunting circulated. Later still, the building was again reincarnated into a museum, but still the whispers of the ghostly phenomena continued. The spirit known for hundreds of years as the White Lady was still making her appearances.

Though only one ghost is known to haunt Old Palace, there are three theories as to who she may have been. The first theory is that she is the spirit of Anna Sidow who was the willing mistress of the terrible ruler known as Elector Joachim II. Joachim was a brutal, unfeeling man who enjoyed the wealth his terrible rule garnered while his people suffered and starved before the palace gates. He was smitten with a beautiful, common woman named Anna Sidow who enjoyed much of Joachim's opulence.

Joachim II did have a wife who gave him legitimate heirs, but he spent much of his time and the country's fortunes upon the vain Anna. Together they reveled in sexual debauchery and seemed oblivious to the suffering of the people.

Anna's actions were so unconscionable that after Joachim II died and his son took over she was imprisoned at Spandau. Exactly why she was jailed is not known, but perhaps Joachim's son saw it as retribution for the misery she had helped to cause the people. Anna died after a terrible few years within the prison walls. According to legends she spoke longingly of her time at the Old Palace and ached to return to it. Some say that since she was denied her wish in life, she made her way back after her death and that she is the White Lady who was occasionally seen.

Perhaps there is another woman, though, who has much more reason to haunt Old Palace for her deeds were truly so monstrous that even time has not obliterated them from memory. During the reign of Margrave Albert, one of the first Hohenzollerns to follow

King Frederick, Albert became infatuated with a young widow named Countess Agnes d'Orlamunde. Margrave Albert was quite the catch for he was not only a wealthy man but he was also very handsome; so handsome in fact that he was known as Margrave the Beautiful.

Albert did find the young widow quite enticing but he wanted nothing to do with her two young children from her marriage. He had flirted with her and perhaps hoped for a dalliance but there is little evidence that he sought anything more.

The story of what happened next has been passed through long generations of Berliners. One day someone pointed out how the Countess d'Orlamunde made overtures toward Albert. Albert carelessly remarked that he would consider marriage to her if he "was not held back by the influence of four eyes." The remark was passed on to the Countess who took it to mean that her young children repelled the king.

Countess d'Orlamunde was beautiful and young but looks would last only so long and she was an ambitious woman. Her mind immediately began to turn toward ways of ridding herself of her children. She could not risk their deaths being detected as murders, so she hit upon a plan to run a thin, long gold hair pin into the top of their heads as they lay sleeping one night. Surely this would not be noticed.

The evil woman slipped into her children's bed chamber late one night and held down each child as she committed her desperate act. In the morning her children were found dead and no one suspected her of their murder.

The beautiful countess began her campaign to win the hand of the king and, of course, her own place on the throne, but she was constantly being thwarted. In frustration, she had to keep her silence. She had murdered her own children so that all obstacles were gone, so why was Albert still not responding?

One day Agnes d'Orlamunde heard from a mutual friend that though Albert still desired to know her more intimately, he felt constrained not to peruse her openly. He had reasons why he could not court her.

The Countess responded by repeating the statement about *four eyes* which she had heard before. But now that did not matter did it? The mutual friend looked at her in puzzlement. Of course, it still mattered. Albert had meant his parents were watching their relationship and did not look upon the young countess with favor. Suddenly a terrible understanding settled over Agnes. Albert had not meant her children were the problem, but rather that his parents were. She had murdered her babies, and all for nothing as she could not become queen if Albert's parents opposed her.

Agnes led a miserable existence after that. She grew more and more unbalanced and died as a mad woman. Her sins were found out and she would eternally be known as the worst type of murderess--a woman who murdered her own children for power and money!

Some of those who had seen Berlin's Old Palace White Lady say she bears a resemblance to the figure of Agnes d'Orlamunde. Is it possible that in death she was cursed to haunt the very building she coveted so much in life?

There is yet one more candidate for the title of White Lady. Many of those who have seen the white lady say she bears an uncanny resemblance to the figure that graces the Iron Maiden in the Tower of the Green Hat. The Iron Maiden was created as a woman in white who wore the Virgin's white veil over her face. It has been theorized that the woman who posed for the creation of the implement of torture has been bound to the building and the Iron Maiden eternally. Is the White Lady the model who posed for the ghastly creation? The truth is that historically speaking none of these three women can be the White Lady, though, they most definitely could be haunting the Old Palace, too. By looking at the history of the haunting it is possible to surmise that most probably the White Lady was someone who suffered at the hands of the royal family. Her visits brought only trouble to the rulers who lived at Old Palace.

The exact name of the White Lady will probably never be known, but there is little doubt that her haunting is fearful and she has become a sort of harbinger for the Hohenzollern family. Many believe that this woman has some connection to France, too, because of the way she responded when France was under attack by Prussia which would later be called Germany.

The first recorded visit from the White Lady was during the reign of John Sigismund. According to the tradition passed down a cocky young page was walking down a hall of the palace when he rounded a corner and was suddenly confronted by the specter of the White Lady. The page had heard of the White Lady and recognized her from the description. The White Lady's face was veiled as she moved toward him. He had been told that if she appeared she should be allowed to pass unmolested and she would not harm anyone, but the page saw an opportunity to prove his bravery. He would be the only one to refuse to move for the White Lady. He stood in the middle of the hall and barred her progress. What did he have to fear from the shade of a woman?

The Lady continued upon her course, but as she tried to step past the page, he reached out and took her arm to restrain her. "Where are you going, madam?" he demanded.

The spirit looked at him from above her veil but spoke not a word. She silently raised a large, heavy key, which has long been believed unlocked the castle rooms, and struck the page hard upon the head. The young man slumped to the floor, dead, and the White Lady stepped over his body as she continued upon her way. At the far end of the hallway two other servants had witnessed the exchange and they hid as she passed by them. Later they would tell the story of the foolish page.

John Sigismund died the day after the sighting. People began to believe that somehow the White Lady was attached to the family. Was she a harbinger of death? History would show that many times the White Lady's visits coincided with some dreaded event in the Hohenzollern family.

After John's death the White Lady was not seen for over one hundred fifty years. Stories of her faded into the mists of time and she had become little more than a scary story to frighten children until during the reign of Frederick William II who was the nephew of King Frederick.

Frederick William II was an aggressive leader who invaded France. His forces took the nation by storm and Frederick William II was soon comfortably ensconced at an inn in Paris itself. He chose the Verdun Inn as his headquarters. Frederick William II one night sent for a certain wine. A servant brought a vintage which did not please him and he decided to go to the wine cellars to choose one for himself. According to Frederick's later testimony, while he was in the cellar his dead uncle King Frederick appeared to him and gave him a warning.

"Call back the Prussian force from Paris, Frederick William," the dead king warned, "Or you shall have a most unwelcome visitor!"

Frederick William II did not understand and pleaded with his uncle to explain.

"The White Lady of Old Palace will come to you unless you remove the troops from Paris. You know what a visit from *her* means!" With this the dead Frederick turned into vapor which hung before the terrified monarch.

In a move that was inexplicable to all those who did not know of the ghostly warning, the king pulled back his troops from France and returned to Old Palace. He would live five more years and never see the White Lady.

The White Lady would become very active in the fall of 1806. She was reported several times that fall. Her first appearance was just before the Battle of Jana where Napoleon was under attack by the Prussian army.

One night King Louis of Prussia was throwing a party to celebrate his victories against the Napoleonic army. He told a young girl to play him one tune for each Frenchman he would kill the next day. The young lady sat at the piano and played until first light. During the night the servants claimed to have seen the White Lady but either King Louis did not know or did not care, for he rode into battle anyhow. He would not live to see nightfall. He died at the battle of Saalfeld, but his successor, Elector Frederick William III heard of the White Lady's sighting and took the warning seriously. He withdrew the troops and left Berlin and Old Palace for fear that the White Lady would call upon him.

Napoleon drove his forces into Germany and took advantage of the superstitious leader's absence to take possession of Berlin. He would live at Old Palace himself for over two months, but the White Lady looked upon him with favor and never made an appearance during his stay.

In 1914 a descendant of the Hohenzollern family was once more claimed after a visit by the White Lady. She was seen in the palace and Kaiser William II was told, but he put no stock in foolish superstitions. Kaiser William II had embarked upon a political course which would actually start World War I. Archduke Frances Ferdinand, a man descended from the Hohenzollern family of the Old Palace, was assassinated in Serbia (now Yugoslavia) while on a diplomatic visit. Many people would say that the death of Archduke Ferdinand would be the final stroke which would seal the fate of the world and start the first world war in history.

The Kaiser, though, did not sidestep the fate the White Woman came to warn the palace about. Kaiser William II suffered a fate worse than death. He was dishonored, lost his kingdom, defeated and exiled to Doorn where he would die as the last ruler of a great line. It was a terrible way for the reign of the Hohenzollern family to end. Worse yet, the death of the last direct Hohenzollern opened up the political field in Germany and helped enable Adolph Hitler to take over only about twenty years later.

There was yet one more brief chapter to the haunting by the White Lady. During World War II Berlin was blitzed with bombs by the Allied Forces in an attempt to bring Germany to her knees. There would have been no better target to destroy in Berlin than Old Palace which was a source of pride for the nationalistic Hitler. The palace was bombed on April 29th, 1945 and it was burned. Some witnesses would later say that the White Lady walked one more time down the halls of Old Palace as the magnificent building burned. Others would agree that she walked but that she did not do so to mourn the burning of the palace but rather that she walked as a warning to a poor peasant man who was then in custody at the Chancellery of the Third Reich. That man, a fellow named Schickelgruber would die in Hitler's custody. Schickelgruber was the last descendant of the Hohenzollern family through it's many marriages. Perhaps Hitler feared that this low-born man could mount a revolt against his government in the name of old Prussia.

There is yet one other theory for why the White Lady walked that one last time.

Some people who knew her history of protecting France said that she walked in silent triumph over the fact that France would now be safe and never again would any Prussian leader attack France.

The history of Old Palace was made all the more fascinating by the White Lady. The mists of history have nearly obliterated the memory of the White Lady of Old Palace, but once she was a force that could make kings tremble.

THE HAUNTED HIGH SCHOOL OF TIJUANA

In the 1940's the Agua Casino was a popular nightspot in Tijuana. After the casino closed the large building sat vacant for several years. There were various ideas about what the building should be used for, but the most practical idea came when the area needed a new high school. The cost of building such a large building was prohibitive, but then someone got the idea to use the casino. It was a building that could be easily modified to suit the new use. The modifications were completed and Tijuana had a new, much needed high school.

A story has built up around the building that stemmed from the school's seamy past. In the 1940's there was a pretty singer who worked at the casino. She was the lover of the man who ran the club. The singer got greedy and decided to steal two small chests in which the casino manager had hidden a great deal of money.

One stormy night the singer executed her plan to steal the money. She knew of the chests but the casino manager had been cagey and had not allowed her to know where they were. Now she needed something to hold over his head, so she poisoned his wine while they were in his office.

She told him what she had done and waved a small bottle she said contained an antidote before him. If he told her where the money was, she said, she would give him the antidote. The casino boss was beginning to feel the effects of the poison, so he told her where he had hidden the chests.

He grabbed for the antidote, but the singer was too quick. Clutching the little bottle she ran from the office. The manager followed her in desperation. He had to get that bottle. The singer, though, had never intended to spare her lover's life. If he lived, he would hunt her down and kill her. Now he would die and she could enjoy her fortune.

The couple ran through the halls of the building. The singer hoping to outrun her lover until the poison took over. It was a desperate chase by all accounts. Suddenly the man pulled a small pistol and took a shot. The singer fell to the floor, dead.

The casino manager died, too, either because the antidote was administered too late or most probably because she had never had the antidote at all. Either way, he must have lived long enough to tell his story before he died.

Shortly after this terrible incident stories began to spread that on stormy nights the apparition of the beautiful singer could be seen. She ran in desperation from a pursuer that no one could see. People said that she ran toward where the money was still hidden. People began to say that if only someone could follow her all of the way, they would discover the money, but no one has ever been able to find it. The ghostly singer always disappears before she reaches her destination. Perhaps she is being punished for her terrible greed by being denied in death the thing she loved most in life--money.

THE MANSION CALLED FAIRACRES

Undoubtedly one of the most colorful and haunted homes in British Columbia is the former estate of Henry and Gracie Ceperley. Fairacres was built in 1909 as a retirement home by Henry who had made his vast fortune as a Vancouver businessman. The house was a masterpiece of architecture. It was a three-story mansion of Edwardian design and no expense was spared upon the construction.

For an unknown reason the property was placed in Gracie's name, and when she passed away in 1919 she stipulated in her will that Henry would be given the right to remain in his home until his death. She further stipulated that upon Henry's death she wished for the mansion and grounds to be sold and the money to be donated to help build and fund the Stanley Park children's playground.

Henry Ceperley had his wife's will thrown out and leased the property to a gentleman named Henry Buscombe. Buscombe would later buy the house outright and would subsequently sell it.

The house would repeatedly be sold and used for various things from a private home to an annex of the Vancouver General Hospital. During this time the home surely saw at least a few persons pass away.

In 1939 the house once again was purchased, this time for the use of the Order Of St. Benedict. For fifteen years the monks lived at Fairacres until a new abbey called Westminster Abbey was completed for them.

Thus ended the honorable years for Fairacres. It was bought by a religious cult called the Society of the Foundation for a More Abundant Life. The cult was run by a self-declared archbishop John I. In fact, Archbishop John I was really a conman criminal named William Wolsey who was wanted by both the Canadian and American authorities. Among the charges against Wolsey were wife beating, embezzlement and extortion. Like so many cult leaders, though, Wolsey told his faithful flock that the charges were trumped up by authorities in order to quiet him and destroy his message. Apparently many folks in the Vancouver area believed in Wolsey and what he was selling, for he had a large following for nearly twenty years.

Those who knew Wolsey said that he was a commanding man who's piercing slate eyes seemed to pin people. He was a tall, well-built man with a gray beard that gave him a Biblical look. He spoke eloquently and with great conviction in a manner which seemed to hypnotize his followers. Wolsey painted a pretty picture of a world in his "church," and he made Fairacres a large part of his plan. Wolsey and his followers used the building and grounds for a church and school. Here, the evil Wolsey manipulated and tortured his congregation. He taught a method called "bio-psychology" which included the use of physical and psychological torture to control his congregation.

Stories eventually leaked out of the church at Fairacres and Vancouver's citizens could barely believe what they heard. One woman confessed to keeping her infant son in a dark closet for months on end because Archbishop John I had told her to. Others confessed to similar acts and worse. Any physical or psychological defect was fair game for Wolsey and he psychologically tortured one small boy who had a speech problem so badly that the child regressed into the mental state of an infant. Others spoke of Wolsey's own private program of teaching personal hygiene and sex to the students. These were classes that only Wolsey would allow himself to teach. He was accused of sexually abusing children and women and of beating them as well. Some of the charges were never proven but many folks felt that everything said of Wolsey and much worse probably happened at Fairacres during those years.

Along with this steady course of abuse, Wolsey taught that he was the only true messiah. He preached that he alone could perform miracles and his devout followers insisted that they had seen such miracles for themselves. There was no breaking the iron control that Wolsey held over his church. In true dictatorial fashion he brooked no arguments. To question Wolsey was to court death. He even taught the children in his school and church that to question or not believe anything which he said would cause their own deaths. He ruled by fear alone.

Of course, it took a lot of money to run such a large operation, and his followers supported him in grand style. He held no outside job, but nearly all of his followers tithed, and some even gave nearly all they owned to Wolsey.

By the end of 1959 people in Vancouver began to seriously question the wisdom of allowing Wolsey to remain. There were many criminal acts purportedly being committed on the grounds of the former Fairacres estate. A local newspaper did a story which exposed some of the unsavory practices of Wolsey and his followers.

For several years Wolsey continued to run his "church" despite the growing opposition to him in the community. He began to see members dropping away from his teachings and he knew that the law was seriously trying to find a way to arrest and convict him without a clamor that they were silencing freedom of religion.

In the 1965 Wolsey stole the $ 2 million dollar treasury of the church and disappeared.

The Canadian authorities and the Americans both have looked for Wolsey but he was never found. (At least I could find no record of his being arrested.)

About a year after Wolsey absconded with the church funds, the Burnaby Council bought the building and turned it into the Burnaby Art Gallery. The gallery remains until this day, and it was the staff of the art gallery which first noticed the haunting.

Some of the former employees and even past curators have described seeing a woman in a dark blue evening dress who has been seen both on the first and second floors. She's glimpsed walking along but does not react to those around her.

There is another spirit which seems separate from the woman in blue. This spirit is that of a tall, thin woman in a transparent nightgown or dress. She is usually seen coming from the third floor area where the children of the cultists were housed. This transparent lady has been seen hurrying down the stairs to the second floor or walking along the second floor by workers. This spirit pads about in her stocking feet and has confounded at least a few workmen who heard her approaching but did not see anyone pass by them.

A pluckish spirit is felt but not seen in the Burnaby Gallery area. It steals tools and moves objects around so that the workers must search for their tools. Often they will find them back in their accustomed places or hidden in remote spots where no one would have been. This spirit seems to be funny and likes a good joke.

Some of the gallery employees have reported an overwhelming sense of pressure or presence which has made them feel they must leave the area. In the mid-1980's one woman claimed that she felt such a strong presence in a rustling dress that it literally drove her from the room.

In 1987 CBS did a special about hauntings which featured Fairacres. They brought in a psychic named Joan Fontaine who pinpointed several haunted areas. At one point during her walk through Fairacres she felt a man push past her who told her he was called Joseph. She also indicated two spots in the basement which she thought were very haunted. She indicated that she heard children crying in pain. Ms. Fontaine was overwhelmed by a sense of sadness and said that these children in the basement were frightened and sad. Perhaps this had something to do with the years when the cult was there.

Unfortunately for those who are actively seeking interaction with spirits, the new management at Fairacres now called Burnaby Gallery will not talk about the ghosts. Perhaps they feel that it somehow lowers the tone of their establishment or perhaps they are just skeptics, but there is no doubt that skeptical or not, people will continue to find spirits at the former Fairacres Estate.

THE HAUNTED OPRAH STUDIO

Oprah Winfrey has many times complained on television about the tabloid press and how it makes up stories about her and other celebrities in order to sell newspapers. Though the lines between tabloid press and the more established press have been blurred throughout the past few scandal ridden years, they still suffer from a lack of credibility in many quarters. However, an article in the National Enquirer from June 29 of 1993 caught my interest. The headline read *"OPRAH'S SHOW IS HAUNTED."* The article caught my interest because I had taped an unusual episode of the OPRAH WINFREY SHOW the summer before. In a total departure for Oprah, she did a half hour segment featuring a couple haunting cases including the Myrtles Plantation. During that segment Oprah had said that Harpo Studio is haunted by spirits that are believed to date from the time of a famous Chicago ship disaster.

At the beginning of the twentieth century the building that is now Harpo Studios was a National Guard Armory. On July 24, 1915 the employees of the Western Electric company and their families and friends happily boarded the steam ship *EASTLAND*, for the company-sponsored, annual day-trip to Michigan City. The *EASTLAND* was only one of five steam ships chartered by the company to carry its 7,000 employees and guests to their annual picnic. Despite it being an overcast and rainy day, there were 2,500 people waiting to board the ship at the North Clark Street pier.

The ship boarding was first come first aboard, and those with a choice picked the *EASTLAND* because it was considered the fastest and safest of the five ships chartered. It would later be believed that the ship's reputation helped lead to the disaster because so many people chose to ride aboard the ship that it became dangerously overloaded before the captain pulled up the gangplank. The steam ship began taking on passengers around 6:30 a.m. and pulled away from the pier at about 7:40 a.m., but by then it was literally filled to the very railings with happy picnickers who were anxious to begin their trip.

As the *EASTLAND* pulled away from the dock, the boat began to list to one side, but the passengers inside the boat did not panic for they were already accustoming themselves to the gentle sway of the ship. The ship listed back and forth for some minutes before it began to capsize. Later a Board of Inquiry would determine that the crew of the steamship had released water from the ballast tanks in order to level out the gangplank to make boarding easier. As they were refilling the tanks prior to moving, the passengers aboard surged to one side of the ship to watch as another ship loaded and this caused the listing to begin. The water in the partially filled ballast tanks began surging as the boat listed badly to the heavily packed side, and this, along with too much weight being badly distributed on one side, caused the ship to capsize.

The ship turned over so rapidly that there was no time for the seated passengers inside the vessel to react. They were thrown violently about inside their deck compartments and were trapped by walls of rushing water. Within seconds the happy day turned into a terrible disaster. People tried to fight their way from the filling compartments but many did not make it. Survivors struggled to pull themselves onto the side of the overturned ship.

Because it was taking families to a picnic, the ship was filled with women and children, many of whom could not swim. The women and little girls were further hampered by heavy clinging dresses which helped drag them down. Despite the efforts of survivors, onlookers and others, 812 people drowned that day. When rescue workers cut into the side of the ship to reach those trapped below decks, they found a gristly sight. The bodies of women still clinging to dead infants and with their children filled the compartments in a sickening display. The men who worked in the boiler room of the ship were also lost. They had literally been cooked alive when the river water had reached the boilers and caused them to rupture.

On what should have been a happy day, the survivors, police, firemen, and passers-by pulled body after body from the river water. The survivors were carried to a nearby store where they were treated and either released or sent on to a hospital. The city of Chicago pulled together to help with the relief efforts. The Red Cross came in within an hour after the disaster and took charge. Doctors who heard of the accident hurried from all over town. Department stores sent blankets, cots and other supplies while the grocery store which became the medical headquarters offered the rescuers any food they could use. Some local restaurants even began sending in sandwiches to feed rescuers and survivors.

Despite the fact that the ship went down only yards from the dock and that it never entirely sank because about 14 feet of one side of the ship remained above water, the devastation to those aboard was terrible. Twenty-two entire families died and nearly one third of those aboard drowned. Nearly every family who boarded that ship with a picnic basket and high hopes that the rain would stop that morning would loose at least one loved one that day. The bodies were carried from the waterfront to two armory buildings. One now houses the Excaliber Club and is reputedly haunted, and the other armory is now Harpo Studios.

The bodies of the dead were laid out in rows of eighty-five and groups of twenty mourners at a time were allowed in to look for loved ones. It was a terrible scene in both buildings and in various other morgues. The devastated relatives wept as they walked along the rows of dead looking for a familiar face among the throng of bloated bodies. It was so traumatic that at least thirty women succumbed to hysteria and mental break down.

Of course, there were also the many curious and morbid people who wished to view the dead. Despite the efforts of groups like the Red Cross, those who sought entertainment by looking at the bodies often made it into the morgues.

With a history like that Harpo Studios would almost have to be haunted. How could so much pain and emotion be spent without effecting the area where the tragedies were played out?

Ms. Winfrey purchased the old building and renovated it extensively as a state of the art television studio. She first heard stories of ghosts from her staff. Editors, producers, technicians and even the janitorial staff spoke of hearing sobbing cries and of seeing different spirit forms.

One form which has been reported often is that of the Gray Lady who is seen in a long dress and a large wide-brimmed hat from the turn of the twentieth century. She is seen floating along past startled employees and does not seem aware of their presence. What's more, the Gray Lady has been seen by guards watching the security cameras at night! She will appear in one camera and disappear before the next camera can pick her up. The crying sound has often been associated with this woman though she is not seen crying. Could she be a victim of the *EASTLAND* disaster or the loved one who had to identify bodies?

There are other, more pleasant sounds heard at the studios, too. The sound of a group of people laughing and enjoying a meal has been heard. One female producer reported to a security guard late one evening that a group of people were in the hall laughing! She had looked out in surprise but though she could clearly hear them, there was no one visible. The frightened producer had called the security guards for help. The guards responded but found no one else in that part of the building.

The sound of children laughing and playing has also been heard in the old section which was once the armory. Could the children who died aboard the *EASTLAND* be playing in their new home at Harpo Studios? Many people who have researched the haunting believe that the sound of children laughing dates back to the disaster aboard the steamship.

Though Oprah claimed publicly not to have ever seen a spirit, it is reported that privately she has admitted to being a victim of the haunting. Items in her office and on her desk are often moved despite there being no one in her office over night. She has had lights turn off when she steps out of the office and she believes that the spirits in the building are turning them off.

Personnel in the parking lot have reported a male spirit which is never clearly seen and disappears quickly. The sound of music from the early 1900's has been heard though no one could find a source. There are also reports of people smelling violet perfume which wafts past them though no one can be seen. The perfume has been associated with the Gray Lady a few times.

Security guards working over night and those who work in the building after hours have uniformly agreed that the Oprah Winfrey building is haunted. From hoards of unseen people tramping past, to ghostly music, the building has more than it's share of haunting phenomena. Ms. Winfrey and her associates have never confirmed the stories publicly, but she has admitted on at least one occasion on national television that her staff believes the building to be haunted and that she believes them.

Paranormal investigator Richard Crowe has been studying the many hauntings of Chicago for nearly thirty years now and he has researched the hauntings at Harpo Studios. He believes that the spirits in the building are associated with the *EASTLAND* disaster and from the one public statement Ms. Winfrey made, she believes that, too.

Richard Crowe hosts "Chicago Supernatural Tours" which offers tours of many of Chicago's most haunted sites including Harpo Studios. If anyone is planning a trip to the Chicago area, a tour with Richard Crowe is recommended. Mr. Crowe can be reached to schedule a tour by writing: Chicago Supernatural Tours
P.O. Box 557544
Chicago, IL 60655-7544
Or by phoning (708) 499-0300 during standard business hours on Central Standard Time.

PRESIDENT LINCOLN AND THE RATHBONE CURSE

April 14, 1865
Good Friday

Twenty-eight year old Major Henry Rathbone looked at his reflection in his bedroom mirror and smiled. He looked quite nice in his dress clothes. He was looking forward to his evening. He and his fiancée, Clara, were going to be spending the evening with the President and the first Lady at Ford's Theater. Henry gave his dark mustache a quick stroke before he picked up his dress hat and hurried from the room. Down the hall he paused as he saw a maid step out of a room and waited until she had closed the door.

"Is Miss Harris ready?"

The young maid turned and nodded. "She'll be out in just a moment, sir. And if I might say so, she looks very lovely tonight." The girl turned and hurried down the stairs. She had to hurry if she would have Miss Harris's wrap ready in time.

Henry proceeded downstairs and into the formal sitting room. He poured himself a small snifter of port and sat down. He was feeling quite proud and happy with his life at present. There had never been anyone more lucky than he. Several years ago his father had passed away and that had been a terrible dark time in his life. But everything had changed a couple years later when his mother had met and married Senator Ira Harris who was a widower. Senator Harris had a young daughter named Clara and Henry had admired her right away. Through the years, though, that admiration had been replaced by love, and now he was gratified to know that Clara shared his feelings. In fact, they were to be married soon.

Beyond that he was also doing well. The president had just appointed him assistant adjutant general of volunteers and young Rathbone saw his future stretching out before him as one long adventure. He was wealthy, rather handsome, talented and lucky enough to be marrying a beautiful woman who also loved him. How could his life get any better? Many young men in his position would have been smug and pompous but Henry truly wasn't. He had much to be grateful for and he counted his blessings, but he was also a very personable young man whom the president liked.

Furthermore, a good part of his festive mood could be put down to the fact that after five long and terrible years the Civil War was over. Only five days earlier General Lee had surrendered at Appomattox and the whole North seemed festive. Even the president had been uncharacteristically happy when Rathbone had seen him earlier in the day. Of course, the President and the first lady were looking forward to a night at the theater. Everyone around the president knew that he loved to go to the theater and that he had been looking forward to seeing the new play at Ford's Theater, OUR AMERICAN COUSIN.

Clara came in and Henry hurried to stand up. All thoughts about the president and the first lady vanished from his mind as he looked at his fiancee. Clara was a petite young woman of twenty years with her dark hair swept up in a series of rolls and curls at the back of her head. Her lovely face seemed to glow with anticipation, but what made her stand out was the dress she had chosen. It was a pure white satin dress with sleeves which dipped off the shoulder and a daring, but demure, amount of decollege showed. Her slim throat was graced by a simple necklace and Henry could not remember Clara ever looking nicer.

"My dear Clara, you are enchanting," Henry said by way of greeting. "I do believe that you will upstage every other woman at the theater tonight."

Clara gave her fiancée a pleased, demure smile. "You don't think the Lincoln's will object?" She twirled quickly which set her dress in motion and Henry could not help smiling.

"I'm sure that the President won't mind being seen with the two loveliest women in Washington City tonight. And as for the First Lady, you know you can do no wrong by her. You've always been a favorite of hers."

Clara waved her hand at him. "It's just that she's good friends with your mother, and Mrs. Lincoln is grateful that I don't believe that nasty gossip that the president's political enemies spread. I certainly wouldn't believe any of that swill that Kate Chase and her set spreads about!" Clara's eyes snapped with the intensity of her feelings.

Henry knew exactly what Clara was talking about. After the Lincoln's lost their little son, Willie, Mrs. Lincoln had confined herself to her room for months. There were rumors that her mind had become unhinged and that she was mad. The president's political enemies had a grand time poking fun and belittling the Lincolns about "Mad Mary," as some called the first lady.

Another enemy as powerful as any politician was Kate Chase the daughter of Treasury Secretary Chase. There was bad blood between Kate Chase and the Lincolns. Though only a young woman, no one ever underestimated Katherine Chase. She was beautiful, cultured, and worldly. Stories of her quick mind and ability to manipulate were legion in Washington City, and everyone knew that Kate despised "that frumpy little woman and her stork of a husband" who had lived in the White House for the past five years.

Kate's father had ran against Mr. Lincoln in the Republican primary and had lost to him. The Chases had come to Washington City, however, when President Lincoln had named Mr. Chase, the former Governor of Ohio, as Treasury Secretary. Kate had taken the city by storm. She held lavish parties, and set the fashion for all of Washington City. Her open snubs of the president and first lady were famous, and it didn't help that Mrs. Lincoln was a difficult woman with some unseemly habits. Still, Henry Rathbone and others did feel that it was at the very least uncharitable to make political hay against a family grieving over the loss of a child. Kate, however, took every advantage afforded her no matter who paid the price.

Clara glanced at the mantle clock and frowned. "I do believe that the Lincoln's must be running late. You did say that the President said they would call for us on the hour, didn't you?" Henry glanced at the clock, too. "Well yes, but perhaps something has detained them. You know the President did ask several other people to attend tonight's performance with them. They all had to decline, but perhaps someone has changed their mind at the last minute. And you know, Mr. Lincoln is still the president. If some great matter has come up he might well have to attend to it before he calls upon us. "But," Henry added with a twinkle, "after he sees how lovely you look tonight, he shall be sorry to have kept you waiting."

Clara gave Henry a warning look. "Really, Henry, you should be a bit more sparing with your praise. A lady might think that it's false."

Henry knew that he had just been put in his place, and rightly so. The end of the war and the chance to spend the night with the First Couple had made his tongue too glib. "I shall be the perfect gentleman tonight, my dear, and you will see that my every word to you was completely sincere." Just as Clara began to respond, the sound of a carriage and team pulling up before the house made her pause.

Henry stood up and offered his arm to Clara. "My lady, I believe our carriage has arrived," he quipped.

Clara took the proffered arm and hurried to the entrance hall. The butler held her wrap out for her before offering Mr. Rathbone his coat.

Henry handed Clara up into the carriage and they settled back into their leather seat across from the President and First Lady.

The President smiled and greeted them both. He complimented Clara upon her dress and Mrs. Lincoln echoed her husband's praise of the dress. The carriage gave a little jolt as the horses began their journey once more, and Clara could not help noticing the sense of anticipation that was in the air.

Mrs. Lincoln and the President were chatting happily about the play they were about to see and about the night. Henry could not help wondering if Mr. Lincoln had sheltered his wife from the knowledge that he had to ask 16 people out for the night in order to get just two. Many people did not like the plump little lady with her odd ways and fits of temper. Clara, however, seemed to bring out the best in Mrs. Lincoln. But tonight it was Mrs. Lincoln and the President who brought the festive attitude to the party. Henry could not remember seeing them more happy or more contented. Mrs. Lincoln took her husband's arm and sighed contentedly as they alighted from the carriage at Ford's Theater and entered. An usher showed the two couples to the President's box in the balcony above the stage. Mrs. Lincoln settled quite close to the President and he indulged her with an affectionate smile and a tender pat on her hand. Clara sat next to the President upon his other side and Henry took up the chair next to Clara.

A hush of anticipation fell over the crowd as the house lights came on and the curtain upon the stage rose. The first players stepped upon the boards and the play, OUR AMERICAN COUSIN, began.

The President and First Lady seemed to grow enthralled as the play continued. It was both absorbing and funny. The president was seen many times smiling and laughed openly as Booth and the rest of the cast performed.

Henry saw Mrs. Lincoln's hand take the President's discreetly and the two seemed almost like young lovers. At a slow point in the play he saw Mrs. Lincoln lean forward and heard her soft whisper. "What will Miss Harris think of me hanging on you so?"

The President's eyes twinkled as he held his wife close. "She won't think anything about it," he counseled smiling. Henry and Clara shared a look that spoke volumes. They were enjoying watching the President and First Lady enjoying the play and each other. There was a brief sound behind them as the door snicked open but no one paid any attention. Before them lay a world of wonder in the play. Booth was off the stage at present but the other players were more than capable of keeping the audience's attention.

Suddenly a movement caught Henry's eye and caused him to jump up and whirl around. A terrible crack filled the playhouse at the same moment, and the audience seemed to freeze. Immediately Henry sprang into action.

He saw the little derringer in Booth's hand. He saw the smoke and smelled the acid smell of spent gun powder. His mind seemed numbed in one respect, but in another way he had never thought so clearly. Booth had just shot the president and he, Henry Rathbone, had to stop the assassin. Rathbone lunged forward just as Booth drew a knife. The two men grappled as Booth fought his way to the edge of the box. Booth welded the knife with precision and Rathbone had nothing to defend himself and the President with but his own body. He fought hard, but the knife licked fire down the length of his arm and he loosened his grip momentarily. It was just long enough and Booth lunged forward and leaped over the balcony railing onto the stage. In that last second Rathbone grabbed for Booth once more and threw the assassin off balance. Booth landed wrong and many there said he seemed to hurt his leg badly in the fall, but Booth recovered quickly and dashed from the theater.

"Somebody stop that man," Rathbone shouted.

Beside him Clara gripped the balcony railing and leaned forward in her earnestness. "Won't somebody stop that man?" she screamed into the crowd.

All around Rathbone was chaos. Mrs. Lincoln was holding the president who had slumped over in his chair. She was screeching loudly and almost unintelligibly. Clara clutched at him, her face covered in a rectus of fear as she tried to attend his arm. Blood covered her beautiful white satin dress but all Rathbone could think of was his President. He had to get help for Mr. Lincoln. He screamed into the audience for doctors--for anyone who could help.

People were now entering the theater box. Rathbone tried to make sense of what was happening. A man who said he was a doctor came in and quickly he began shouting orders. Someone tried to take hold of Rathbone and attend his wound but he pushed the man away.

"You must see to the president," he muttered as he followed the entourage across the street to a house.

At this point Rathbone was glad to see others taking over but he could not bear to leave the President. Had the assassin killed his dear leader or was there reason to hope?

Men in evening dress led Mrs. Lincoln, who was sobbing uncontrollably, into a parlour. Clara followed closely behind, looking ashen.

"Henry, you've been hurt. You must let a doctor look at that arm." Clara tried to hurry from the room, but Henry's hand on her arm stayed her progress. "No, they must see to the President first," he commanded. He saw the fear in Clara's eyes and softened. "It's not as bad as it looks, Clara."

Clara insisted that he at least allow her to tend the wound and she tried to stem the flow of blood with her silk handkerchief. Her hands and face were covered in blood and her once pristine dress had terrible splashes and smudges of scarlet.

Despite his confident pose Henry was not feeling so strong. Shock and loss of blood were making him woozy and he thought that he had better sit down before he dropped. Everything seemed to be moving so slowly and his sense of distance seemed off. How on earth could the sofa be so far away from the fireplace suddenly?

Henry realized that he was collapsing upon the floor but it was a detached sort of knowledge. Clara gave a cry of shock as he left the haven of her arms and went somewhere in the black distance that was quickly taking him over. He heard terrible moaning and ragged sobs and knew that Mrs. Lincoln was still crying.

Clara clutched Henry's limp body and screamed for help. She had never been so terrified in her whole life. She felt that she was in the middle of a nightmare that she could not awaken from. The President had been shot in the head, her dear Henry was unconscious in her arms with blood bubbling out in a terrible way. Mrs. Lincoln was beyond reaching with words at the present, and if someone didn't do something soon she might join Mrs. Lincoln. Someone had to tend to Henry and get the blood to stop or else he would die.

She screamed for help again thinking that there was entirely too much blood.

People came rushing into the room. A man pulled on Clara's arms as she held Henry and she allowed him to slip away. The man was saying that he was a doctor but he seemed frightfully young to Clara. There was another man whom the doctor gave her to as he began to probe the wound. Quickly he tore the sleeve of Henry's jacket and dress shirt. The sight of her Henry's arm laid open in a terrible gash from nearly shoulder to elbow made Clara sick, but she refused to give in to her nausea. Someone had to stay alert and rational. Someone had to answer questions and make decisions and it seemed the task had been left to her.

The young doctor worked upon Henry; Clara averted her eyes. In a corner she saw Mrs. Lincoln sitting. The little woman looked like a wraith in her dark dress. Her hair was disheveled and streaks of blood splattered her in a few small places. Though Clara, did not know it, she looked far worse.

Mrs. Lincoln made a terrible keening sound as she rocked back and forth. Some of what she cried was unintelligible but she would lapse into periods where she kept moaning, "They've killed him. Oh, they've killed my husband."

A gruff voice seemed to float out and reach Clara in her nightmare. "Someone shut that damned woman up."

Clara knew that the voice meant Mrs. Lincoln and she stumbled over to the First Lady. She took Mrs. Lincoln's hands and pulled them away from her face. "Mrs. Lincoln, you must calm down. For the President's sake please calm down." Clara's voice was at once both comforting and commanding and Mrs. Lincoln seemed to respond. She nodded and pulled her hands away. "They've killed him, haven't they, Clara?" she whispered.

"We don't know that yet," Clara said. "There are doctors in the room working on him. Perhaps we should be praying for a miracle."

Mary Lincoln nodded but she seemed incapable of movement. "My Willie was taken, and so many in the war, and now they've taken my husband, too."

Clara glanced over at the men and saw a table upon which sat an assemblage of liquor bottles and glasses. She hurried across and poured a small draught. Going back to the First Lady she pressed it into her hands. "Please drink this. I've heard it will help steady you."

The First Lady took the glass in numbed fingers but did not drink. Her attention was elsewhere. Clara turned and followed Mrs. Lincoln's eyes. The men were moving Henry to a sofa. His arm was swathed in bandages and he was still unconscious. Without saying anything to the ladies, the men left. They returned to the President's bedside.

There seemed to be a great deal of activity in the house. Men were coming and going. Political figures as well as doctors and even reporters made their way around the house. Clara satisfied herself with sitting near Henry and with watching the First Lady who had once more entered her own tortured world.

At one point Clara saw Robert Todd Lincoln, Mary's only remaining son, bending before his mother. Mary Lincoln had begun sobbing loudly again and collapsed into her son's arms. Clara offered her help as Robert tried to get his mother to her feet. "Perhaps she'll quiet if she sees father," he told Clara, as they helped his mother to his father's bedside. Mrs. Lincoln seemed to come alive with grief when she saw her husband. She tore away from Clara and Robert and threw herself upon the prostrate Mr. Lincoln. Men wrested her away and pushed her into a chair. For a time she sat quietly holding her husband's hand and sobbing. Clara returned to Henry and waited.

Soon she heard terrible cries from the bedroom where Mr. Lincoln lay and she recognized the voice of Mrs. Lincoln. A man shouted, "For God's sake get her out of here." Mrs. Lincoln returned to the parlour but she was hysterical. Clara stood up to help Mrs. Lincoln but the First Lady recoiled. She stared at Clara aghast.

"Oh, my husband's blood, my dear husband's blood!" she wailed, flailing with her escort. Clara looked down and for the first time realized how much blood she had on her. Though surely some of it might have been the President's, she knew that most of it belonged to Henry. With the dawn came the news that the president had died. The word assassination would haunt the country forever. Henry recovered enough to be moved and Clara returned home with him. She took off the hated dress and washed blood from her face and hands before falling into bed.

In the weeks that followed Henry recovered physically though not emotionally. Mrs. Lincoln left Washington City a widow without even a pension to sustain her and her remaining son. Clara traveled to her family's summer home outside of Albany, New York. She took with her the terrible memories of the night President Lincoln died and also the white satin dress she had worn. Somehow she could not bring herself to part with it, nor could she bear to have it cleaned. It was a part of what had happened and she felt compelled not to destroy it even though she could not bear to look upon it. She instructed her maid to cover the dress and hang it in the closet. There Clara would let it hang.

A year passed and Clara no longer thought much about the dress. Her concerns were with Henry who seemed to have been plunged into a world of darkness. He had never forgiven himself for not saving the President. He was now a darker, more brooding man than the one to whom she had become engaged.

Clara returned to Albany before the first anniversary of President Lincoln's death. The anniversary night of the assassination arrived and Clara could not help thinking about it. She tried not to brood, and went to bed and fell fast asleep. A sound in her room roused Clara. She lay in the darkness straining to hear it again. The sound came again. Laughter low and soft. She knew that voice; had heard that laugh before. It was President Lincoln's laugh and it was coming from her closet. Bewildered and frightened Clara listened for it to come again. Lincoln laughed softly just as he had in the seconds before John Wilkes Booth had shot him.

In the morning Clara told her family of the experience, but they tried to brush it off. She had been upset they said. She had been thinking of the president before retiring and had dreamed of him. It was all perfectly simple and logical, but Clara knew better. She had been awakened by President Lincoln's soft laughter and it had come from the closet where she had hung the white satin dress.

Another year went by and this time the Harris family had guests over the anniversary of the death of President Lincoln. A guest was staying in Clara's room that night. In the morning their guest came to breakfast with an odd story to tell. The person claimed that in the night they had been awakened by the sound of low masculine laughter coming from the closet. The family remembered Clara's story the year before but said little.

Clara and Major Rathbone were wed in 1867, two years after the terrible night in Ford's Theater. They had three children but their life was not a happy one. Henry slowly descended into insanity. He blamed himself for Lincoln's death and he became increasingly unpredictable. The Rathbones began a series of trips to various doctors looking for help for Henry. He complained about many physical problems, he suffered from horrid delusions, and was besieged by paralyzing fears. Three years after they married Henry had to resign his military commission and he pursued help for his deteriorating health full-time. They traveled to Europe looking for spas or doctors who could help.

Through the years an abiding fear that Clara would abandon him seemed to take root. Henry grew increasingly paranoid and possessive. Clara grew to look upon that night when President Lincoln died as the beginning of a curse upon her family and Mrs. Lincoln. Robert Todd Lincoln had been forced to have his mother committed to an insane asylum because she had been acting alarmingly bizarre and he feared for her safety.

Through the years the Rathbones had returned to Albany, New York from time to time for visits at their summer home. Clara had the closet with the white satin dress in it entombed. It was shut up and covered over with brick so that no one would ever know that it was there. After the Rathbone's visit to Albany in 1882 the family sat off once more for Europe in the never ending quest for help for Henry. Christmas morning of 1883 found them no better off. Henry had slipped completely into madness, though Clara could not admit it. Henry suffered terrible, debilitating headaches which left him prostrate. Early that morning he came to Clara's bedroom and told her he wanted to see the children. She put him off by telling him that it was too early to awaken them. Rathbone seemed calm and relatively normal. He had dressed and was calm.

The sound of voices roused the household and a terrible bang made the maid and a member of the family the Rathbones were staying with hurry to Clara's room. There they found Clara shot in the head with a revolver. Rathbone hacked at himself with a knife and managed to inflict six wounds. Clara died but Rathbone survived. The coincidence of the events did not escape Clara's family and friends. Rathbone had reenacted the event in the box at Ford's Theater which had altered the course of his life. Clara was buried in Germany and Rathbone was placed in an asylum. He would live out his life in paranoia and delusions.

The Harris house outside of Albany was rented out. People reported that a shot was often heard in Clara's room on the anniversary of Lincoln's death and people who stayed in the room over the anniversary date reported seeing Lincoln coming from the closet or a young woman in a bloody white dress crying pitifully as she emerged from the bricked up closet. When Henry died in 1911 it seemed that the curse begun that night in Ford's Theater had been fulfilled. Everyone had paid a full measure for that night. Clara murdered, Henry mad, Mary Todd Lincoln cast into obscurity and near desolation. The white satin dress was all that remained. The stories of the dress and the room surfaced from time to time and a book was even written about it in 1929.

Perhaps the dress would have been forgotten if not for Clara's son, Henry Riggs Rathbone who became a United States Congressman. Henry Riggs was destined to spend his life dealing with the legacy of Booth's hateful act. In 1910 he had the wall of bricks torn down so that his mother's dress could be retrieved. He believed that the dress held a curse which had destroyed his family. Henry Riggs took the cursed dress and burned it.

He would propose in 1928 that Ford's Theater become a museum to commemorate Lincoln's assassination and the theater remains today as it had been on April 14, 1865, in large part because of Henry Riggs.

If the dress was cursed, it would claim one last revenge upon Henry and Clara long after their son destroyed it. In 1958 the German cemetery where they were buried dug up their remains and destroyed them because the graves were so long forgotten and untended. Thus ended the lives so promising that night the young couple had accompanied a President and his lady to a theater for a bit of entertainment. Not one vestige of Henry and Clara was left untainted by the cursed dress and the destiny that seemed to be Lincoln's.

THE GHOST OF GILLAN'S WAY

1810

At the best of times justice can be rough, but when passions are heated and hearts inflamed by a terrible crime, often the wrong conclusions are drawn and justice is denied. There is a story from Scotland, which has bothered the honest folks of Lhanbryde for nearly two hundred years. Was an innocent man murdered? Is that why his spirit is still seen on a little tow-path known even to this day as Gillan's Way?

On a foggy night in August of 1810 10-year-old Elspet Lamb disappeared on her way from her family's little farm to the village of Urquhart about two miles distant. Throughout the long night her family and their friends searched the path for her, but she was not found. At first light dogs were brought in and they lead the searchers to a tangled mass of bushes on the Muir of Stynie where she was found. The poor child's head had been smashed open and nearby they found a pair of men's work pants which were covered in her blood.

The bloody pants quickly lead to a local fellow named Alexander Gillan who worked as a farm hand on a local farm. The pants looked like his and folks immediately recognized them.

Young Gillan had come to the village from Ireland, and there were those who did not like the foreigner. Others claimed that he was not quite right in the mind. He was a timid man who seemed a bit simple in his ways.

Gillan was found at the local church at the end of a prayer service for the young girl. He had known the Lamb family and had romantic feelings for Elspet's older sister, but the girl cared little for young Gillan.

Gillan was quickly and roughly arrested at the church and taken to the larger town of Inverness for trial. When he was arrested he was wearing his "best breeks," (pants) and no one bothered to see if his other pair of pants were at his home. They assumed that the ones they had were his, and proceeded upon that premise.

Gillan's fate seemed to be sealed when it was known that he'd be appearing before Lord Justice Clerk to the Scottish Sessions, Charles Hope. Hope had a chip on his shoulder against commoners because he had once been one, but saw himself as better than the locals now. He was a brutish man who was often extreme and cruel. His punishments were often far more severe than those meted out by his contemporaries. It had been intimated that his fellow judges held him in contempt, but he had ingratiated himself with the wealthy and powerful by doing their bidding.

Young Gillan was terribly frightened and, being a bit simple was completely at a loss when it came to his own defense. He went to trial and had no chance to speak for himself. According to the records, throughout the trial poor Gillan clutched a bit of paper upon which he had scribbled a few words of defense. However, he never had a chance to read them at the trial.

The prosecution insisted that though the pants had not been positively identified as Gillan's, who else could they belong to?

Gillan listened as he was painted as a cold-blooded murderer who had brutally killed a young girl. Further, they insisted that he had molested the child. Still he waited for his chance to speak in his own defense. Gillan never was allowed any time to speak on his own behalf. He was quickly found guilty and sentenced.

Charles Hope turned upon the hapless Gillan and spewed out a ten-minute speech denouncing the young man, condemning him to death by hanging and to perdition after that. He reportedly said in part, "...it is decreed that a criminal such as you shall be bereft of all burial and that his body shall not be permitted descent into its Mother Earth like those of Christians. I have resolved to make you a lasting and memorable example of the fate which awaits the commission of such deeds as yours."

The fate Charles Hope decreed was extreme and cruel. He said, "I have therefore determined that after your execution you shall be hung, suspended in chains until the birds of the air pick the flesh off your body, and your bones bleach and molder in the winds of heaven..."

Poor Gillan was taken by cart on the appointed day of November 14th back the forty miles to the Muir of Stynie where young Elspet had died. Gillan was weak with hunger and starved nearly to death for he had been given nothing but bread and water since his arrest. It was nearly dusk by the time the strange procession arrived at the scaffolding that had been erected for the occasion.

Gillan, again clutching the same paper, was roughly shoved up the scaffolding. He must have known by then that his fate was sealed, but even then he waited for his chance to offer his last words. He wanted to read the words he had written before he was killed, but even now Gillan would not be allowed to speak. The rope was forced over his head and he was quickly dispatched from this earth. Those who witnessed the execution said that he only lost his grip upon that little scrap of paper as his body swung. Unheeded, the paper floated to the ground where it was not retrieved. It seemed that no one cared enough about Gillan's words to even read them after his death.

Even death was not enough to satisfy the judge. As soon as Gillan was declared dead, his body was cut down and placed into a strange cage of metal in the shape of a man. He was strapped into the cage and re-hung from the gibbet where he had died. There poor Gillan was left to hang and swing eternally.

The day after the hanging some people came to view the body and returned to the village with a strange tale. Though the metal cage still hung swinging, Gillan's body was missing. It appeared that someone had not agreed with the harsh verdict, and had taken down the young man's body and given it a burial in some secret place.

Folks would also say that for days the paper Gillan had held blew across the ground as if beckoning someone to pick it up and read it. Supposedly no one ever did.

For years the gallows and the metal cage hung along the little path that became known as Gillan's Way. The rusted iron cage groaned and squealed in the winds and folks for miles around grew accustomed to the sound of the gallows and the terrible cage rattling and squealing, but it was an unnerving sound. In 1911 the gallows was finally removed and under them the skeletal remains of a man was found. It is believed that the bones were Gillan's.

The story of Gillan would have died away with the mists of time if Gillan had remained quiet, but Gillan is a restless soul. People have seen Gillan along the path where the gallows were ever since shortly after his death. He stands and stares at them quietly before fading into the mists.

Even today folks speak in hushed tones of Gillan's Way. It is now part of the Crown

Land and is in the care of the national Forestry Commission. Even the local forestry service officers respect the story of Gillan's spirit haunting the little road. In *Mysteries of Mind Space & Time*, a forestry worker is quoted as saying, "...the place worries me simply because you never see deer or a bird there: a hundred yards away, yes, but that place is always deserted."

Speculation about Gillan's guilt still swirls in the area. Does he haunt the path because he was an innocent man? One story claims that Gillan was guilty but that he had never intended to hurt Elspet. He had loved her older sister who had teased and spurned him. He had thought it was she walking through the mists that night and had gone after her. He had been shocked and terrified when he realized that the girl in the mists was Elspet and not her sister. He had killed her then.

How could anyone know such a thing? Was it possible that someone had read Gillan's scribblings upon that scrap of paper after all? Was that what he had planned to say? Since Gillan's ghost has never spoken, we can only speculate upon what keeps him earthbound.

THE BEST LITTLE RESTAURANT

From time to time I receive letters in response to ads I've placed or from folks who have read my other stories. I received one that left me with an interesting question. Can real people eat at a phantom restaurant and not know it? Apparently that is what happened to Clifford Porter and his wife.

Clifford Porter and his wife were visiting Spokane, Washington state when one evening they decided to look for a place close to their motel to have dinner at. They found a little place which they went into.

The restaurant was quite nice, if a bit "homey." It was crowded and hazy with smoke but it looked like a popular place. You could tell that the restaurant had been open a long time. The couple sat down and took the menus offered by a waitress.

"Oh my," Mrs. Porter said looking at the menu. "How do they stay in business at these prices?"

Mr. Porter was staring in surprise at his own menu. The price list for the meals was more than reasonable. He had not seen prices like that for years. Well that helped explain the popularity of the place. Prices like that were something to return for, but he hoped that the food would be good.

They discussed what they would order, and decided to have steak and eggs. The waitress came and took their order. While they waited to eat, they looked around the busy little restaurant. The clatter of glasses and cutlery mingled with the chatter of the customers. The couple chatted and sipped their drinks. They looked around at the other customers. This little place could have been called "a greasy spoon" yet it must have been one with a long established reputation for good eating.

Soon the meal came and despite the low price it was wonderful. The meat was cooked to perfection. The eggs were done perfectly. The couple ate and finally the waitress returned with the check.

Mr. Porter frowned when he looked at the check. The young waitress had made a mistake on it. The price she charged was slightly different than the menu prices.

"Excuse me," Mr. Porter called to the waitress as he waved her back. "I think you made a mistake on this check. The price for steak and eggs in the menu was more than that." Mr. Porter liked a bargain as good as the next fellow, but he was not one to take undo advantage.

"I don't think so," the waitress began. She took the check and left. A few minutes later she returned. "Thank you," she smiled. "I'm sorry. You were right but it was our mistake. You pay the price we charged you and not a penny more," she insisted.

The Porters paid their bill and left. They talked about the little restaurant on the way back to the motel. It was a place they would like to visit again before leaving Spokane.

The next day the couple decided to visit the restaurant again. They went back to the street and found the building but something was very wrong. Where the night before a busy, noisy restaurant had been, there was now only an empty building.

Puzzled the couple tried to find an explanation. Could they be in the wrong place? No, the rest of the landmarks were very familiar to them. This was definitely the place where they had been the night before. But how could that be? The building had obviously been empty for some time. There was no way that it could have been closed down overnight without any trace of the restaurant being left!

The couple returned to their motel still trying to figure out the mystery. They had eaten in that building the night before but how could they have? They tried looking for the restaurant's name in the phone book but there was no such listing.

The Porters would never really have an explanation for their mysterious evening out. They would eventually divorce, but they would always agree upon the events in Spokane where they had supper in a restaurant that did not exist. To quote Mr. Porter, "The building was vacant the next day... It never existed, except for us..."

This story alone would make an interesting story, but it does not need to stand alone. There are many other stories of people who visited diners or restaurants which did not really exist. Perhaps the most famous example of this were the four friends on vacation named Len and Cynthia Gisby and Geoff and Pauline Simpson who were traveling through France on their way to vacation in Spain in October of 1979.

The two couples had difficulties finding a motel on the main Montelimar Nord auto route, but in Dover they found an old hostel sitting back from the road. It was after 10 p.m. at night and they were tired. They parked their car and gratefully entered the hostel. Inside they were treated to old world hospitality and a charming atmosphere from another era. They felt comforted by the homey establishment.

The affable landlord spoke no English so conversation was at a minimum, but the two couples rented rooms for the night and inquired about food. Soon they were sitting down to a meal of eggs, steak, chips and tankards of lager. Even the meal had been served upon what looked like antique plates.

After the meal the couples went to their separate rooms. There they were surprised by the authenticity of the old-world surroundings. The beds were very high and were bolstered instead of using pillows. There were old-fashioned heavy blankets and sheets. The windows had wooden shutters but no glass. The heavy wooden doors were fitted with wooden latches but there were no locks. The bathroom had an ancient shower and a strange soap attached to the claw footed tub by an iron rod. Later the couples would say, "We weren't all that bothered because everything was very comfortable and, being in rural France, we just thought that was the way of life there."

The next morning the couples ate a lovely breakfast and just as they were getting ready to leave a young lady entered the room followed by two gendarmes. The officers uniforms seemed odd. They were dressed in old-fashioned uniforms with high hats, capes and garters. The lady wore a long dress and buttoned boots.

Len spoke to the officers and asked directions back to the auto route. The officers were confused by the word auto route even though Len was sure he was saying the word correctly. The officers did recognize the town Avignon and gave them directions to it. Len offered to pay the bill for their stay and meal but was shocked when he was told that they owed only 19 francs or roughly the equivalent of three American dollars. Len had expected to pay about 250 francs but the landlord insisted that he'd accept no more than 19 francs.

Back in their rooms Len and Geoff took pictures of their wives before the shuttered windows.

After a lovely vacation the Simpsons and Gisbys began the return trip back home. When they neared Dover once more, they decided to stop again at the hotel. To their surprise they could not find it. They took the same turn off the auto route and found a tree-lined street just as before. The advertisements upon the walls of the buildings, the other buildings themselves, were all just as they remembered. Everything was as they remembered it, except that there was no hotel. The entire structure was gone; even the parking lot where they had left their car previously.

The two couples had no choice but to take rooms in Lyon which cost them 47 francs, but they could not stop thinking about their stay in Dover. Nothing about it made any sense.

The couples were even more mystified when they received their packets of developed film. Every picture they had taken of their holiday had turned out--except those taken in the Dover hotel. It wasn't that the pictures were cloudy or the negatives black. There were no negatives and no ruined photos. It was as if they had never taken any pictures in the hotel rooms.

A few weeks later the couples made another trip to Dover in hopes of clearing up the mystery, but they still could not find their hotel.

Later the Gisbys would describe the clothing of the gendarmes and the lady in the long dress to a French dressmaker they knew. The woman told them that the uniforms and the dress had to be from the early 1900s. The dressmaker said that the uniforms they described had not been worn by the gendarmes since 1905.

What did happen to the Gisbys and the Simpsons? Had they somehow stepped back in time and entered a world that no longer exists? Even so, what about parking their car in a place that now was a brick wall. How could two material objects exist in the same space? One can only wonder about what happened to these two couples and one can only speculate about what happened to the Porters in Washington state. The very idea of a time slip opens up many questions which no one in this world is qualified to answer!

THE LAST GOOD-BYE

It was early in the afternoon as Carl Sypolt walked down the street. He nearly passed up the funeral parlor as he passed it, but something made him stop. Inside lay the body of a fellow he knew not particularly well, but the dead man had been his barber. Carl paused outside the silent building; perhaps he should go inside and pay his respects. He had known the man after all, and it was only the polite thing to do.

Carl pulled open the door of the funeral home and stepped in. The building was slightly darkened and very quiet. It had that peculiar smell of formaldehyde and flowers, which is universal to such places.

There was a placard with the barber's name on it and Carl entered the room. The room was empty except for the rows of folding chairs that sat vacant, the softer couches and chairs against the walls, and the casket in the front of the room. The casket was opened and flanked on both sides by banks of flowers. Carl was slightly surprised to find the room completely empty but perhaps the family had needed a rest. Loosing a loved one was very traumatic.

Carl caught sight of the sign-in book on its little table at the back of the room and hurried over. He would sign his name so that the family would know he had come to pay his respects.

Well, Carl thought, while he was there he'd just go up and look at his old barber. Carl felt a bit sad for the family of the dead man but he was not overly sad himself. He had only lost a barber, not a friend.

The body looked quite nice the way the funeral director had laid it out. Carl paused for only a minute and just as he began to turn away something caught his sight at eye level, beyond his reach, about six feet away. As Carl stared up at the wall above the casket, it seemed that a tiny two-inch square window of light appeared a couple feet from the top of the wall. Carl was taken aback. He had never seen such a thing. The little window was surrounded with blackness and something about this little window frightened and yet held him pinned beside the casket.

As Carl watched, the dead man suddenly appeared in the window. Carl could see him clearly from the top of his head to his waist. The dead man appeared alive and smiled at Carl. The barber lifted his left arm and waved casually as if to say "so long." For a brief second Carl almost returned the gesture, but he couldn't quite do it.

The vision lasted only a second or two and was but a brief glimpse to Carl, yet he was completely sure it had happened.

For Carl the most difficult part of the experience was finding a way to put it into context with his Pentecostal beliefs. Carl wrote to me, "...it is important to me that experiences harmonize with the Bible.

"A theory I like, is one that explains that the fallen angels can and have masqueraded as friends and relatives from the past. Having been in existence before mankind, they have at times, imparted historic facts that would lend "proof" of reincarnation and deja vu. Everyone isn't saved, therefore, many who experience a clinical death and return with a good report, have been duped. At the same time though, there have been those who were saved, and the experience was authentic."

In a subsequent letter he added:

"The visitation in the funeral parlor was Browning's Funeral Home in Kingwood, WV. There was no detectable change in temperature. There was no fear and no time to get surprised when the vision appeared...I felt an impulse to return the "so long" gesture, and later felt regret that I had not done so. I was happy to have received such an experience..."

Did Carl experience a trick by an evil spirit or did he witness an old acquaintance saying his last good-bye? You must judge for yourself.

NELLY BUTLER'S RETURN

Throughout history there are certain stories which have captured the imagination of society. These stories are told and retold repeatedly until they become a part of the fabric of the culture, yet there are other stories which for some reason are consigned to the back pages of the history books or to the back shelves of academic societies. These stories are often more spectacular and better documented than the popular stories, yet they are not well known. What forces come into play to make this so I do not know, but I began wondering about that when I first heard of Nelly Butler and realized that she had a story to tell which has only rarely been heard. I believe this is an amazing story in the annals of hauntings, and after you've met Nelly and heard her story, you will, too.

August 9, 1799

Abner Blaisdel lived between the villages of Machiasport and Machias in Maine. He owned a farm where he was raising a thriving family. By all accounts Abner Blaisdel and his family were God-fearing folks who never asked for nor expected what was about to occur in their home. It was August 9th when the voice started speaking to the family.

Abner was frightened of both the disembodied voice and the idea that his neighbors along the coast would hear that spirits were in his house. Fearfully he warned the family not to mention what was happening in their home. He prayed that God would banish the voice and hoped that the spirit would leave them all unharmed. The voice called out the names of the family members and asked to speak to David Hooper. It claimed that it was Hooper's dead daughter.

For a short time it seemed that the voice went away and Abner undoubtedly breathed a sigh of relief. It was good to believe that God had answered his prayers, but the voice returned on January 2, 1800. It had only been gone for approximately five months.

Once more the female voice began talking. It again said that it was Nelly Butler, the dead wife of a local man named Captain George Butler and asked once more for her father, David Hooper to be sent for. The Blaisdel's had known Nelly Butler and they knew both Captain George Butler and David Hooper.

After a couple days of having the voice repeatedly request that David Hooper be sent for Mr. Blaisdel sent two messages to David Hooper asking him to come to the Blaisdel farm. The Blaisdels were frightened of the voice which ordered them to do it's bidding. They were frightened, too, that if they did not listen to it the spirit calling itself Nelly Butler would harm them.

David Hooper read Blaisdel's first note and tossed it in the fire. The second letter imploring him to come angered Hooper. It was all a terrible waste of time and the whole idea that his Nelly had returned from the dead was the worst foolishness David Hooper had ever heard. Still, he saw that he'd have no peace until he answered the Blaisdel's letter and went to put a stop to the insanity that had apparently taken hold of the entire Blaisdel family.

David Hooper appeared grudgingly at the Blaisdel house. It had been a six-mile ride and it had not been very comfortable in January! Hooper was furious by the time he arrived at the Blaisdel house and he was ready to denounce the whole thing as either a fraud or a hoax that was blackening his dead Nelly's name and memory.

Everything changed for David Hooper the moment the Blaisdel's welcomed him into the house. As the old man warmed himself by the fire, a voice suddenly spoke behind him. "Father, I am glad you're here!" David Hooper whirled in shock. He knew that voice well. It was the voice of his Nelly who had only been dead a few months. She had died during childbirth and soon after her death they had lost the wee baby as well. He had been devastated by his losses, as had his son-in-law, George. David Hooper had never hoped to hear Nelly's voice again, but now he had just heard it. There was no mistaking the voice and David Hooper began a conversation with the disembodied voice that convinced him that this was his Nelly. He asked the voice questions that only he and Nelly could have answered, and in each instance without any hesitation the voice answered in great detail.

When David Hooper left the Blaisdel home that day, he was thoroughly convinced that he had just spoken to his dead daughter. Later David Hooper would write an affidavit in which he stated, "such clear and irresistible tokens of her being the spirit of my own daughter as gave me no less satisfaction and admiration and delight."

The Blaisdel family was not as enthusiastic about Nelly's visit. They were worried about the spirit and concerned about what the younger children were feeling. They certainly did not ask for the spirit to come to their home and they would have gladly seen it gone. However, that would not happen. Instead, Nelly decided to do more than just talk to her reluctant hosts.

One evening Captain Paul Blaisdel, Abner's son, was walking through a field on his way home when he became aware that a woman was in the distance. It was late in the afternoon on a cold January day and he was puzzled about something about the woman. Although he could clearly see her, she appeared unreal somehow. He watched her closely as he walked along and soon he realized why she seemed a bit "unreal." He had known Nelly Butler before her death and this woman was she. The longer he walked along, the more sure he was of the identity of his companion. Suddenly Nelly seemed to turn toward him and came rapidly toward him. Paul realized that this woman was gliding along just above the ground instead of walking. At an impossible speed Nelly approached Paul. She paused before him but spoke not a single word. In dumbfounded silence Paul stared back at the woman hovering before him. He would later say that he was struck by how very white she appeared. While Paul struggled with himself to overcome his awe, Nelly simply vanished before his astounded eyes.

Paul hurried the rest of the way home and poured out his story. His father counseled him to pray and warned the family again lest they let word of the "Spectre" should leak out to the neighbors. He greatly feared their reaction to a "Spectre" living in his house and pursuing his children through the fields.

Paul struggled with himself about the sighting and tried to rationalize it away. He was a ship's captain after all, and he knew that sometimes things were not as they seemed. He knew well about hallucinations and tricks of light and shadow that made an ordinary object seem quite different.

The night after the sighting Paul was still at home and the family was all at home from the youngest children to the adults. Paul and the family were in the setting room during the evening when suddenly a light appeared and Nelly stood there. The entire family witnessed Nelly's appearance. She turned and looked at Paul who was frozen in his seat. "Paul Blaisdel, why did you not say hello to me in the field yesterday? Do you no longer pass the time with friends and neighbors?" Nelly demanded in a cross tone. Before Paul had a chance to stutter an answer Nelly vanished.

Once more Mr. Blaisdel sternly warned the family to avoid speaking of the "Spectre." They tried to avoid the subject and hoped that Nelly would simply go away. They little needed a ghost that rebuked them and demanded they produce family members for it.

The end of January came and no one saw nor heard from the "Spectre." February also passed without incident and the Blaisdels breathed freer. Perhaps the bizarre incident had passed away with no one outside the family any the wiser. Their hopes would prove futile, though, for in March, Nelly returned to the Blaisdels.

One raw March day Nelly simply appeared in the house where some of the family had been gathered to work. Nelly's voice came from the air before the startled family.

"Hallelujah! Hallelujah! Hallelujah! Hallelujah!" she said by way of greeting. "I have returned to you. You will please go to the cellar where we shall talk. Go now, please!"

The insistent tone of Nelly's voice coupled with the sudden fright made the four Blaisdels compliant and they reluctantly went into the dark basement. Before them they heard Nelly's voice.

For nearly two hours Nelly chatted away about life and death and Heaven and her place in it all. "Though my body is consumed and turned to dust my soul is as much alive as before I left the body." She told them at one point.

It was a strange conversation for the Blaisdels. They sat in the blackness of the cellar talking to an invisible spirit that wanted to chat cheerfully. Though the family would have rather been almost any place but the cellar; they were too frightened to refuse the "Spectre" any request and stayed as long as she wanted to talk.

Nelly did not return after that until April. This time she made several visits to the Blaisdels. She visited the family a total of six times and talked about life, Heaven, and her family and even indulged in a bit of gossip. She always spoke in religious terms, however, and began and often ended her conversations with strings of "Hallelujahs."

By now Mr. Blaisdel's worst fears had begun to materialize. Word spread that the Blaisdels were haunted by the specter of Nelly Butler who had appeared to them once and often came as a disembodied voice that spoke at times for hours. People were both curious and suspicious. Some folks wanted to witness Nelly for themselves and came to the Blaisdel house, while others muttered that this was Satanic and that the Blaisdels had obviously done something to draw out such a spirit. Many of those who heard Nelly speak vouched for the fact that it was certainly Nelly's voice, but others noted that this "Nelly" was quite religious whereas the real Nelly, though a church goer, had not been especially pious.

Some of those who came to hear Nelly also saw her for she began putting in appearances when friends and family along with the curious came to call. Interestingly, Nelly would appear in a room where several folks would insist they saw her while others in the same room at the same time insisted that, though Nelly spoke, she never appeared. Were people hallucinating, or did Nelly appear in such a way that only select people could see her? This became even more controversial because some people could not hear Nelly speak either. In each group that came it seemed that some saw and heard her, others only saw her, some only heard her and yet others saw and heard nothing. This made the story of Nelly very controversial.

Perhaps one of the oddest parts of the haunting was that even those who could not experience Nelly often returned. Soon many of those who had been skeptical because they had not seen and heard her began to say that they now could. After several visits to the Blaisdel home they claimed that Nelly took pity on them and allowed them in her presence.

Those who did see Nelly always described her in the same way. She was a figure in bright white that shone all around. She did not appear as a dead woman, but seemed to glow from an Inner Light. When she appeared to folks in a field near the Blaisdel home, they said she lit up the field with her bright light. Others insisted that she lit the Blaisdel's basement so brightly that they needed no lantern to see by.

The basement seemed to be a favorite spot for Nelly. She often insisted that her visitors seek her out in the basement. There she held court. The Blaisdels, however, were expected to provide food and drink for the curious and they were growing ever more tired of Nelly's hospitality. But the Blaisdels were in a delicate situation. If they dared to turn away anyone, they might be accused of creating a hoax, so they granted one and all access to their home and cellar and tried to be good neighbors and hosts. Because people often traveled from a distance to see and hear Nelly, the Blaisdels were forced to offer lodgings. There are no accounts of them charging for food or for lodgings. It seems that they were afraid to turn anyone away or to ask for help with the expense of feeding and sheltering so many. At times over a dozen guests would be staying at one time.

A woman named Mary Gordon came from the village of Machiasport on August 4th of 1800 and stayed with the Blaisdels. Mary told the family that she had come to see Nelly's ghost and she was not disappointed. Mary wrote about her visit with Nelly and described it in detail. About two hours before dawn (about four o'clock) she claimed a terrible flurry of loud knocks roused the house. They all hurried into their clothes and rushed downstairs. The Blaisdels knew that Nelly usually announced her visits with a series of loud pounding noises that nearly shook the house.

Downstairs the family and the many others the Blaisdels had allowed to stay to visit Nelly hurried to the basement. Mary wrote that there were approximately twenty people in the basement that morning. The basement was black as Nelly began her visit only by speaking. The people sat in the darkness and listened. Mary later described it thusly, "I heard such a voice speaking to us as I never heard before nor since. It was shrill but mild and pleasant."

"Mr. Blaisdel, in addressing the voice, said that several persons (of whom I was one) had come from a distance to obtain satisfaction, and desired that she would tell us who she was, and the design of her coming."

Nelly told them her maiden name and that she had married Captain George Butler. She spoke of her various reasons for coming back and as she spoke a shimmering light grew in the midst of the gathering. At first the light was merely a bright mass but it changed to form the shape of a woman. Mary wrote that the group stood in two rows around the light so close that they could have touched her. Mary described the experience in her journals; "We stood in two ranks about four or five feet apart. Between these ranks she (Nelly) slowly passed and passed again, so that any of us could have handled her. When she passed by me, her nearness was that of contact; so that if there had been a substance, I should have certainly felt it. The glow of the apparition had a constant tremulous motion. At last the personal form became shapeless--expanded every way, and then vanished in a moment."

A minister named Abraham Cummings heard of Nelly Butler's specter and he was appalled at the trickery that was being wrought upon the good people of Machias and Machiasport. Cummings was a graduate of Brown University, a very educated man who was well known in academic circles for his devout faith in God. His belief was so strong that he believed God would provide whatever the minister needed as long as the minister continued to do God's work. In 1793 Cummings had ministered in the Bath, Maine area and had filled in for a local Congregational Church until a permanent minister could be found. In payment for his work Cummings was given a sailboat. Cummings saw the sailboat as a sign from God that he was to travel about ministering and he commenced to do just that. He sailed the coastline preaching from his boat in dock areas and in local churches when he was invited. It was while he was preaching in a little church in Machias that he first heard the story of Nelly.

In order to combat reports of the "Spectre" at the Blaisdel home that was now famous for miles around, Cummings planned a sermon on the evils of superstition. He chastised the congregation for believing in false doctrine and warned them about the dangers of believing in something so obviously not biblical as ghosts. When Cummings left Machias, he felt that he had dealt with the "Spectre" thoroughly.

In June of that year Cummings was once again sailing along the coastline and put in at Machiasport. He accepted a temporary post as minister at a local church. He once again heard stories of the Blaisdel "Spectre" and spoke out against such nonsense. He was growing greatly grieved by what was happening in the area.

By July Rev. Cummings was growing increasingly frustrated with the stories of the ghostly Nelly Butler, which were infiltrating his church. Some of the congregation came to church one night gossiping that the "Spectre" had returned to the Blaisdel farm. The gossip spread through the church and Rev. Cummings decided to take matters into his own hands. He would go to the Blaisdel farm and confront this bogus specter and put an end to this superstitious foolery once and for all!

That night Rev. Cummings thought of his plans as he walked home. He saw a knoll ahead of him with a group of white rocks protruding in the distance. He sniffed. "That ghost is probably some such thing. Just something these superstitious folks have mistaken is all. A good dose of common sense is what's needed!"

The Reverend kept walking along toward the knoll. He looked down to choose his step along some loose turf and when he looked up a couple moments later he came to a dead stop. Before his very eyes one of the white rocks was rising. It separated itself from the group and seemed to be floating toward him. The white rock was changing shape and was turning a rosy color. Rev. Cummings compelled his legs to continue onward. Reason must prevail!

He took only a few steps toward the light when he realized that it was taking the shape of a woman. He never looked away nor blinked lest the woman of light might simply vanish, but rather he continued toward it resolutely. By now he could see the figure clearly and, though it appeared to be a woman, she was very tiny. The diminutive form was hardly larger than a child at first.

The Reverend stopped and stared. "You're too small to be the woman who has been appearing among the people," he fleetingly thought. As if in answer to his thought, the figure shifted and grew until it was the size of a woman. Light burst around her and illuminated her. When Reverend Cummings later wrote of the miraculous event he said, "...she appeared glorious with rays of light shining from her head like a halo extending clear to the ground."

Rev. Cummings remained still as he watched the woman of light. He felt fear but tried to banish it. At the same time he felt a strange elation. It struck him as odd that the two emotions had burst over him together, yet he clearly noted that they did. He spoke not a word for he seemed to remember reading somewhere that when confronted by a spirit it should be allowed to speak first.

The "Spectre" seemed to stare at Reverend Cummings but she remained silent. With a flash she was instantly gone. Reverend Cummings found himself quite alone upon the knoll. Something within the Reverend had changed. This had been his epiphany. From that moment forth he would become not only a believer but also Nelly Butler's best witness. Reverend Cummings set about searching out and recording the eyewitness testimony of every person he could find who claimed to have seen or heard Nelly's ghost. He would examine every claim and write of his own experiences at the Blaisdel farm. All of his investigations would be put down in a report that he would publish. He would go on to write a pamphlet about Nelly Butler which he published in Bath, Main in 1826, only one year before his death. A copy of that pamphlet still exists at Brown University. Another edition of the pamphlet would later be printed in Portland, Maine in 1859 and three subsequent printings would appear. Unfortunately for history, Reverend Cummings, though by all accounts an excellent minister, was not a good researcher or writer. His accounts often were vague. To save space Reverend Cummings used only abbreviations when interviewing and this made checking his stories very difficult. He also forgot to give the location of the Blaisdel house and the dates of the interviews and sightings. He took great care to report faithfully the witnesses words but neglected other facts entirely. He often made vague suggestions and made assumptions that were difficult for any reader not very familiar with the story to understand.

Reverend Cummings would one-day write that he only wrote his pamphlet "to present to the public a complete, satisfactory analysis of this whole mystery." He seemed intent upon clearing the Blaisdel name. The Blaisdels were inevitably accused of fraud because the specter appeared in their home. They were also suspected because eventually their daughter Lydia and Captain George Butler (Nelly's husband) would marry.

As Nelly's appearances grew more numerous, the Blaisdels grew more frightened. The younger children were terrified of the entity and moved into their parents' room. They took to sleeping in groups and lived in fear of the knocking or the voice shouting "hallelujah," which were Nelly's calling cards.

In response to this fear Nelly took action. She did not want to frighten children and she spoke to them. "Be not afraid--you not be. I never hurt you, did I? And I shall not hurt you not. Put your things in place." Nelly confined herself to the cellar and outside. Comforted by Nelly's words and her voluntary banishment to the cellar, the children eventually returned to their own rooms.

Nelly then turned her attention to other matters. She had worried about her husband who still grieved for her and their lost child. She spoke to him as well as other family members who came to the Blaisdel home. George Butler was completely convinced that the "Spectre" was his dead wife. He later wrote, "When I called to talk with this voice, I asked, 'Who are you?' It answered, 'I was once your wife.' The voice asked me, 'Do you not remember what I told you when I was alive?' I answered, 'I do not really know what you mean.' The voice said, 'Do you not remember I told you I did not think I should live long with you? I told you that if you were to leave me I should never wish to change my condition; but that if I were to leave you, I could not blame you if you did.'"

George Butler knew that this conversation had occurred in their home when they were alone and no one else could have known of it.

Nelly appeared to George several times as a figure in a "winding sheet." Several other people saw her at those times.

Nelly fixed the idea in her mind that it would do George good to have a new wife and she selected Lydia Blaisdel whom she knew George had once admired.

Abner Blaisdel was upset by the ghostly matchmaking. He wanted Lydia to have nothing to do with Captain George Butler. He wanted no further links to the Butlers since Nelly had settled there. Lydia, too, balked at being matched up with her future mate by his ghostly wife.

Captain Butler began coming to the Blaisdel home shortly after his father-in-law, David Hooper, confirmed that the "Spectre" was truly Nelly. During the months that followed Captain Butler renewed an old attraction for Lydia Blaisdel. Captain Butler knew that Lydia's father did not approve of him as a match for his daughter, but at times Lydia encouraged the relationship discreetly.

However, once Nelly began telling Lydia that she should marry George Butler, Lydia grew angry. George Butler proposed to Lydia after his dead wife apparently gave her blessing but this only angered Lydia more.

Lydia and George Butler had a terrible row during which she adamantly refused his proposal. Why, George wanted to know?

Lydia was furious. "I'll not marry any man who had to be frightened into proposing to me by the ghost of his dead wife!"

Captain Butler continued to woo Lydia and assured her that Nelly's urging only coincided with his own feelings of love for Lydia. Eventually Lydia changed her mind and agreed to marry George Butler despite her father's continued opposition.

The announcement of the impending marriage between Lydia and George Butler caused a furor in the nearby towns. People began to whisper that Lydia was somehow behind the odd visitations from Nelly. They said that Lydia had cleverly faked the entire series of events in order to bring George Butler to her home where she hoped to renew their old romance.

Lydia was stung by the criticism and speculation of her neighbors. Everywhere she went she was pointed out and whispered about. She grew utterly wretched and miserable. At last she decided to break off her engagement and go away. She broke the news to George Butler and gave him back his engagement ring. George Butler was furious about the gossip for he knew Lydia to be an honest and honorable person, but he was also very hurt. He pleaded with Lydia to change her mind and pointed out that their marriage must have been divinely ordained or else Nelly would not have come back to bless it. No words could sway Lydia. She had been hounded so badly that the gossips were driving her from her own home.

Lydia booked passage aboard a ship that was to soon leave Machiasport. She hoped to travel down the coastline to a town far away where she could start a new life, but that was not to be. Only days before Lydia was to leave home for good, Nelly paid the family another visit. The curious were also present and they all heard the voice warn Lydia that leaving was futile. Reverend Cummings would later write, "the miraculous voice solemnly warned her (Lydia) in the hearing of several witnesses, that her efforts were in vain, and that her affliction would sail with her."

Lydia again changed her mind and sent word to Captain Butler that she would marry him. Soon after that a very small, private wedding was held.

Only days after Captain Butler and Lydia were married Nelly appeared in her former home. She warned her husband, "Be kind to Lydia, for she will not be with you long. She will have one child and die within the year." Nelly faded as she whispered her warning.

George Butler was shaken by his dead wife's prediction. Ten months later Lydia died only one day after giving birth to her first child.

Nelly not only warned her husband of his second wife's death, but she also warned others correctly about events to come. Once she predicted that the Blaisdels would be dragged into a legal battle that they would eventually win. They were sued but did win in time. After this Abner Blaisdel received a letter from his family in York, Maine which was over two hundred miles away. In the letter he was told that his father had fallen mysteriously ill. In desperation Abner asked Nelly if she could tell him what ailed his father and how they could help him. Nelly replied, "Hallelujah, I am from above, praising God and the Lamb. I am a voice crying in the wilderness bringing light to those I can. It is too late to help your father. He has been called away. I am sorry he has died." A few weeks later word arrived at the Blaisdel house that Abner's father had passed away. He had died before Nelly gave Abner the news.

More than once people who had known Nelly in life came away questioning this religious Nelly who liked to intone "hallelujahs" and often opened or ended conversations with praises for God and the Lamb. At one point Abner asked Nelly about this. "I did not know that a person's very nature changed so upon death. How is this so?"

Nelly replied that her nature had changed as she lay upon her deathbed. She called for her parents and reminded them of their last conversation before her death. They had been trying to comfort her about the loss of her babe and she had spoken of the child resting with Father God and the Lamb. Her parents confirmed for all that during her last living day, Nelly had experienced a profound change of spirit.

The gossip mill ground on relentlessly and Lydia was the focus of it all. People claimed that Lydia somehow threw her voice using ventriloquism in order to make the sound of Nelly talking. They claimed that Lydia dressed in white clothing and appeared as Nelly. They whispered that the two women were not seen together. This bitter talk grieved Nelly and she began to speak up on Lydia's behalf. She warned groups of witnesses who had come to see her that Lydia had no part in her appearances. She spoke in defense of the Blaisdel family and once even ordered two women to remain with Lydia in the kitchen while she appeared to a group in the cellar. In this way she hoped to clear Lydia's name.

Another time Nelly ordered a group of visitors outside for a hike. She told the group to march two by two "as at a funeral." The group began to march along with Nelly's glowing form clearly bringing up the rear. Nelly insisted that Lydia be her partner and the two walked together for approximately two miles before Nelly called a halt. "I have done this to prove that Lydia is not assuming my shape," she told the audience.

Not everyone believed that Lydia was causing the haunting. Many folks who had witnessed the strange events believed that the entity was not Nelly Butler but was a demon sent from the devil. Chief among the supporters of this theory was Nelly's own sister, Mrs. Sally Wentworth. Sally had been persuaded to come to the Blaisdel home on August 8th of 1800. She later wrote, "I was there with about thirty others and heard much conversation. Her voice was still hoarse and thick, like that of my sister on her deathbed, but more hollow. Sometimes it was clear, and always pleasant. A certain person did, in my opinion ask her whether I was a true Christian. The reply was, 'She thinks she is she thinks she is. She is my sister.'

In another passage Sally Wentworth described a conversation between her and her sister before Nelly's death. It was a private conversation that Nelly spoke about. This shook up Mrs. Wentworth until she speculated, "Could not some evil spirit hear that conversation, and afterwards personate my sister and reveal it?"

The entire family was stigmatized by those who felt that they had done something to bring evil upon their home. People wondered what the crime was for which they were punished by having to entertain evil spirits?

One of the things Nelly insisted upon was having her dead child's body dug up and re-interred approximately thirty feet away from the original grave. She gave no reason for this other than to say that in time they would know all. Reverend Cummings wrote of this and indicated that eighteen months later everyone understood why Nelly needed to have the infant's grave moved, but Reverend Cummings failed to mention the reason for the benefit of his readers.

Nelly eventually stopped appearing and her voice quieted forever, but not before literally dozens upon dozens of people had witnessed her amazing feats. Many skeptics came away convinced of the reality of the haunting and many of them swore out affidavits about what they had seen. There has never, to my knowledge, been any single haunting witnessed by more people than that of Nelly Butler. She was an intelligent, compassionate, and witty spirit who constantly gave her opinions and exhibited secret knowledge.

I could not help being struck by some likeness to the Bell Witch of Tennessee and the Livingston entity that haunted a family both in Pennsylvania and West Virginia in the late 1700's. Yet Nelly was completely different in other respects. She clearly identified herself and came not to browbeat and terrorize the family, but in order to set to rights matters that had been left unsettled at the time of her death. Inadvertently her appearances did harm the credibility of the Blaisdel family, but eventually Abner and the family grew to have a philosophical attitude toward the haunting and the suspicions that the family had faked it. He once told a skeptic, "You must think as you please. I am clear, and I believe my family is." The visitation of Nelly Butler was unique and beyond question unless one wishes to believe that dozens upon dozens of people including ministers who had come to debunk Nelly were all fooled!

THE VOICES

Do the dead speak to the living in order to bring comfort or to pass on messages? Throughout the years I've received many letters from sincere people telling me of disembodied voices, usually of loved ones, which have spoken to or helped them in some way. Historically speaking, this is a very common occurrence. Throughout time people have come forward with stories of dead family members who have spoken messages of warning, comfort and love to the bereaved.

Among the letters I received was one from Mr. Porter which told of an incident which had stuck with his sister and himself for years.

His younger sister, Julie, had several supernatural experiences throughout her life, and she seemed to pass this knack to discern the spiritual on to one of her daughters.

Mr. Porter wrote to me:

"When our own father died in 1978, Julie was sleeping in the car, while her husband and I went in to eat at a buffet place a mile from the hospital. Dad appeared to Julie in the car saying he was sorry he was not a better father. He could not accept her reassurances otherwise, then she said "you loved my mother" and then he was gone..."

Julie noted the time, 7:15 p.m., and later learned that this was just when their father had passed away.

Sometimes these voices offer protection or give warnings, as a letter from Mr. Sypolt indicates:

"I was driving alone, back to Cleveland, Ohio in December of 1959. By daylight I became very sleepy and still had about sixty miles yet to go. I fell asleep and instantly from the passenger side of the car, came an audible voice (it sounded like my father who was still living at the time) in a very weary tone. "Don't go over twenty-five miles an hour, Carl." The voice awoke me, and I had to look over to make certain I was alone. I don't believe the message per se was of any significance, but it was audible words to excite and revived me and kept me awake in wonder."

In a letter responding to my questions, Mr. Sypolt explained his view of the above incident while driving home in his 1952 Chevy during the early morning hours:

"I do not believe it was my father, but (the voice was) of a guardian angel."

Later on Mr. Sypolt spoke to his father about the incident and asked if his father had been thinking about him traveling at that time. His father's response was cryptic:

"A few months later, on a return visit home, I mentioned the experience to my father who was still alive at the time. He merely chuckled, and the subject was changed without his offering of any possible thoughts of me at the time it happened."

How could Mr. Sypolt's living father have spoken to him? Was it telepathy or just his subconscious giving him a warning in a voice he would respond to?

The idea that the dead talk to us has long fascinated me, and I was truly struck by the following story.

Air Force pilot, Richard Bach walked along the beach in Monterey, California trying to forget his troubles. It was 1966 and he had been unable to find work as a pilot in the civilian marketplace because there were a lot of military pilots looking for work. Bach was depressed because he was not even able to earn a decent living writing about flying for the aviation magazines. His family finances were growing desperate, but there upon the beach he could walk along in the anonymous fog and listen to the calling of the sea gulls. He envied those birds who gracefully swooped along the skies without a care in the world. They could fly as he longed to, yet no longer could.

As he walked along, the fog thinned, and he could see that he was alone on the beach. It was a lonely, yet quiet world with just the surf and the birds to keep him company.

"Jonathan Livingston Seagull!"

Bach froze. Who was that who had said that name? He whirled about looking around, but there was no one there. The birds continued to dive and swoop above and the surf sang it's familiar song but Bach saw not one being capable of speech. The very idea of disembodied voices spooked Bach who turned back and hurried to his house.

In his home he went to his room and sat down. He knew how strange his experience was, but he felt compelled to address the voice. "I don't know if you're really there, voice, but if you're really there I don't understand what you mean. If you're trying to tell me something, explain it to me."

Suddenly Bach felt a rush of images fill his mind. He had never had any such experiences and he grabbed up a pen and paper to record the images. He felt compelled to record what he saw. He just knew that he was to write about this.

Bach began to scribble as rapidly as he could. The story unfolding before his mind's eye suddenly stopped. Bach felt a terrible frustration, as if he had gotten engrossed in a movie and was stopped from viewing the pivotal parts.

Weeks went by as Bach read and re-read the scribbled pages trying to figure out what should come next but he just could not continue the story.

At last Bach tucked the pages away and went on with his life. Months later he moved to Ottumwa, Iowa. Bach was still writing about flying and aviation and now he had developed a fascination for seagulls. He wrote that sea gulls needed to improve their flying techniques.

By now more than a year had passed and, though he still thought about that voice in the fog and the subsequent vision and story, he had given up upon finishing it.

One night Bach had a strange dream in which it seemed he was back in the world of his vision in California. His dream picked up just where the vision had stopped and now he witnessed the ending of the story of Jonathan Livingston Seagull, a bird driven from his flock.

As soon as the dream ended, Bach awoke and hurried to his typewriter to finish the story. This story became a best-selling book and movie. Bach would receive many accolades for his story, but Bach never believed that it was truly his story. He believed that this story belonged to another, and he was just the instrument used by the voice to record the tale.

As the story grew to prominence, some people recognized the sea gull's name. There was a real Jonathan Livingston who was a pilot who had lived in the 1930's. This Jonathan Livingston was an aircraft designer and a racing pilot who had been a bit of a dare devil during his life. Jonathan Livingston, the man, died prematurely when his plane crashed. Was there a connection between the dare devil bird and the dead pilot who would have understood Bach's frustrations and desire to be in the air once again? Did the dead pilot give a fellow pilot a helping hand when he needed one? Bach would never have an answer to his question, but he would always be grateful to that voice which changed his life.

There are many other stories of disembodied voices which have changed lives, and I'll pass along one more personal account which is credited with saving a life.

This woman I'll simply call "Sharon" and she wrote:

"...I was working seismic. It was winter time & I was trying to drive up a fairly steep hill with a big 4 wheel drive truck & I kept spinning out. So I would back down the hill & try again. I finally got to a point where I said to myself, alright, one more time & if it doesn't work I'll have to go around the long way. So, I proceeded up the hill again & spun out just about the same place I'd spun out several times before. I applied my feet to the clutch & the brake & suddenly the motor stalled. I began to slide backwards. The brake no longer worked with the motor stalled, nor did the steering wheel. I quickly decided that maybe I should jump out & just let the vehicle go. I opened the door & was thinking that I needed to get up & over the door, otherwise it would grab me on my way out & perhaps do some serious damage. I was just getting ready to go out the door when suddenly a voice screamed in my ear- NO!!!!!!!!!! I was quite surprised & decided that maybe jumping out was a really bad idea, so I closed the door & rode backwards down the hill in the truck. I was really frightened & felt quite powerless. It turned out to be quite benign because the truck didn't gather much speed because the hill was not that big. It kind of veered off to the left backwards & banged into a tree & came to rest there."

Could it be that the dead are speaking to us all of the time but we only rarely catch a phrase or a sentence when they see we're in intense danger? The practice of EVP (electric voice phenomena) tends to indicate that the dead are talking but we humans are just unable to listen. Furthermore, there are psychics throughout the ages who have claimed to hear the voices of the dead. For centuries they have been celebrated and reviled by various groups. Could it simply be that they are hearing voices of the desperate dead who are anxious to communicate with the living. This is a controversial topic at best, and each person must make up their own mind. Indeed, even many who experience such phenomena don't know what to make of the voices, but many others who have heard them do believe."

THE WILLOW SALOON

Did you ever *feel* that there was just something wrong with a place? It just seemed that the very site drew evil to it? There are places around the world like that and in northern California there is such a place. That site is now home to the Willow Steak House, but the history of this ground is drenched in blood. The total of known deaths on this site are thirty-four.

The earliest recorded history of the site mentions it as the site of a public lynching. After the hanging there were four more known violent deaths on the same ground. When gold was discovered throughout California, Jamestown was no exception. A mine ran through the site and gold was taken from the Sierra Madre foothills, but something else would happen in Jamestown.

The small community was destined to be forever marked by an event that happened there in 1862. The town was then a mining town filled with the rough and tumble of risk-taking men and the desperation that drove others into the terrible, dark, dangerous mine shafts after gold.

Late one afternoon the town heard a tremendous explosion or boom, and they realized immediately that the terrible sound had come from the mine. People ran from all corners of the town to the disaster area. They worked feverishly through the first night and on into the next day, but there was no chance for the men below. At last it became obvious that no one would survive the mine collapse. Twenty-three men had been buried alive.

Within a few days of the collapse plans were made for a building to be put on the site. The Hotel Willows was erected there, but from the day the hotel opened people whispered that it was haunted. How could it be otherwise when the very ground beneath had stolen twenty-three lives?

The hotel was the scene of at least six more deaths. In the 1890's the hotel was owned by a couple named Sims. According to contemporary reports, Mr. Sims shot his wife, Elualah, to death in the bar. Since that time the spirit of this red-headed woman has been seen repeatedly.

In 1925 a man named Gus Radu or Rado owned the hotel and bar. One day he called his wife up to their apartment and there he shot and killed her before turning the gun on himself. Why he did this is not clear, but the hotel had seen two more people die.

Two more people would die in one of the three major fires to destroy the Willow Hotel. No one has slept in the building for over fifteen years, but that has not completely stopped the fires. Through the years numerous smaller fires have erupted in the building.

There is not much information available about the genesis of the haunting, but a legend has built up around the building that the mine shaft that lays one hundred feet beneath the hotel had collapsed because the men had accidentally cut into a tunnel that led directly into hell. People say that demons or Satan himself travels that tunnel to the earth above.

It was a fanciful notion at best, or at least the very idea seemed fanciful until 1896 when a terrible fire raged through the area. The whole of Jamestown was becoming engulfed, and the water supply was being exhausted. Someone came up with an notion to dynamite several buildings in order to change the course of the fire and save the hotel. The men set the dynamite in the buildings which had been evacuated and soon they began the explosions. What they did not know was that a man was inside of one of the buildings and that man was killed in the explosion. A relative of the dead man was infuriated by the way his family member died. He vowed that he'd burn down that damned hotel himself!

As the years went by, the irate relative nursed his grudge until he finally died. People would have forgotten the man and his hatred of the hotel if not for the fact that after his death the hotel seemed to be suddenly fire-prone. It was destined to burn the sleeping area three times.

A terrible coincidence about the fires became obvious and people began to remember the man's vow to burn the hotel down. On July 21, 1955 the hotel caught fire and burned. On July 21, 1975 the hotel burned for the second time. Once more it would catch fire on July 21, 1985, and this time the fire would cause damage that was estimated at $200,000. This time the family who owned the hotel decided not to rebuild the second floor. Instead they spent their money and time on the first floor restaurant. They named the remaining building the Willow Steak House and it is still open today.

The steak house is now the center of the haunting. Kitchen staffers report that containers fly across the room and other items move about mysteriously. Lights turn on and off by themselves. The ceiling fans have a mind of their own, and the smell of fire can still be caught from time to time. People talk about hearing terrible screams, men shouting, loud bangs and thumps and even the sound of fire roaring around them. But perhaps the most unnerving part of the kitchen haunting from the staff's perspective is that of the laughter. Several times staff members have heard someone laughing loudly in the kitchen only to hurry into the room because they supposed that the kitchen was empty--and it was. Yet they clearly had heard the loud laughter!

A terrible, demonic laughter has been heard in the restaurant ladies' room as well. One guest, Vicki, heard the sound of a maniacal evil laughter echoing through the bathroom one night. Terrified she ran from the room and decided not to return to the restaurant again. But a while later Vicki did return with a friend and they took photographs throughout the building. In one photograph of Vicki there is a reddish shadow in the darkness behind her. The shadow clearly appears to be of a man with a large hooked nose and horns in silhouette. People say he looked like the devil.

The guests and bar staff have reported seeing men in the building, particularly in one certain booth. The men who are seen appear to resemble the classic idea of a miner. They are older, have scruffy faces and wear battered hats. Some folks have reported seeing a short, balding man walking the halls; and still others report seeing a man who wears a black suit and looks like a gambler sitting at the bar.

The balding man was actually held responsible for the one fire. Local newspapers ran a headline **"Fires prompt psychic probe 7 Ghosts 'registered' at Hotel Willows séance,"** another headline read, **"Did Ghosts Set Fires?"** and yet another headline pertaining to the hotel's flame-loving entity read, **"BALDING GHOST BLAMED FOR FIRES AT HOTEL."** Is this "balding ghost" the spirit of the bald-headed man seen in the building?

These headlines are not just idle speculation to sell newspapers. They were prompted by eye witness reports that a balding man was seen at the source of one fire. The man just faded away. After the 1975 fire several witnesses came forward to say they saw nine entities hovering amid the flames while the building burned. Who or what they saw remains a mystery.

The Mooney family purchased the building in the 1972 and have owned it since. They have heard all about the hauntings at the hotel through the years, but Kevin Mooney was a skeptic until he related an experience he had several times for documentaries and news stories about the haunting. Kevin claimed that one winter evening a man in a trench coat and dark sun glasses entered the bar where he was working alone. There were no other customers so Kevin and the man struck up a conversation. The mysterious man began asking questions about the building being haunted. Kevin admitted that it was and told a few stories about the many experiences in the building. Still the man probed deeper, asking more questions, and Kevin began to feel very uneasy. Something about this man and his demeanor unnerved Kevin.

Finally Kevin decided he had had enough of his customer. He told him politely that he was going to close up. The customer laughed and asked if Kevin was scared. Kevin was scared and admitted it. Still, the man got up and quietly left. Kevin was glad.

Quickly Kevin cleaned up and shut things down. He turned out lights as he headed for the kitchens in the back of the building. Just as he was about to go out the back door he looked up and saw two red eyes looking through the glass. The red eyes blinked at him and Kevin was immediately terrified. He turned and ran for another exit, but it seemed jammed. Kevin pried on the door until it opened and he ran outside. He did not see anything outside in the darkness, but those horrible eyes and the mysterious customer had frightened him badly.

Through the years banging and other sounds were often heard. The day of a fire in 1985 the employees kept smelling smoke. They located the source and called the fire department. After the fire was put out the firemen determined that there were no wires or other flammable items in the wall that could explain the fire. The source of the fire remains unknown.

Mr. Mooney asked a few firemen to stick around in case something else would happen and they did. One fireman claimed to have been one of a group at the bar to hear terrible scratching beneath the floor and unexplained thumping at the waitress station. This phenomena frightened the fireman and he decided to go outside to get away from the unnerving sounds. As he stood on the hotel porch, he heard two distinct, loud sighs emanate from the wall directly behind him!

Stories of the haunted hotel and restaurant brought a local television crew to the building. They set up cameras and spent the night. They also brought still cameras and took many photographs. One person saw a man disappear from in front of a booth. Quickly the reporter took a picture of the booth and claimed to see two transparent men in the photograph when it was developed.

The crew reported having a great deal of difficulty with the equipment. The machine kept switching to black and white from color and there was a great deal of electrical static on the film. At one point the walls seemed to be shaking and the camera filmed during what appeared to be a mild earth quake, however, there was no earth quake nor tremors that evening. The crew felt cold spots and reported other phenomena commonly associated with the haunting. Perhaps the most unusual part of their experience occurred when they tried to view the tape at their home. The machine would flip off repeatedly and even ejected the tape by itself several times. They have had difficulty getting the tape to play despite the fact that it was a new tape and the VCR played other tapes well.

During the 1990's psychic and paranormal investigator Nick Nocerino and paranormal investigator Chuck Pelton investigated the hauntings at the Mooney family's request. They determined that the building was haunted by at least nine entities. Mr. Nocerino tried to free the spirits but he claimed that several refused to leave.

It appears that there are at least three "layers" of hauntings which accounts for the many types of hauntings experienced at the Willow Steak House. It is as if the layers of emotion are being peeled back at random to reveal glimpses of the building's dramatic past.

The Willow Steak House does have a fascinating past even without the stories of the many hauntings. It hosted President McKinnley and outlaw Bart Masterson once stayed there as well. It was a building of historical significance and today is a lovely restaurant. Anyone who enjoys a good meal would do well to spend some time at the steak house. Of course, the management can't promise a ghostly experience, but they do provide a mighty good steak!

> *The Willows Steak House can be reached by phoning (209) 984-3998. It is on the corner of Willow and Main streets in Jamestown.*

THE HAUNTED STUDIO

The building that now houses an ABC studio where STAR SEARCH and THE MOMMIES were filmed actually has a rich history. It was originally the Earl Carroll Theater when it first opened in 1938. Here major Hollywood stars of the day like Jack Benny, Milton Berle, and Errol Flynn came to party. They loved the night life of this dinner club with its burlesque shows. Carroll's show included up to 60 male dancers (many who were 18 years old or under) who would from time to time dance nude. This was frowned upon by the local authorities who repeatedly raided the establishment and arrested Carroll.

The stories of Earl Carroll's night club were legion and, of course, there were many tragic tales to tell. Young dancers committed suicide or were murdered in the club. This atmosphere was rich with emotion and chaos.

The Earl Carroll Theater was shut down and later reopened under new management as the Moulin Rouge and later still as the Aquarius Theater in the 1960's. Here shows such as the Rocky Horror Picture Show were put on.

After that the building sat empty for a while before it was purchased by ABC TV. It has seen much use as a part of the ABC studios, but along with new ownership has come a resurgence of activity. Marilyn & Caryl--The Mommies taped both a talk show and their brief sit-com from that stage. George Hamilton and his ex-wife Alana taped their talk show, the GEORGE & ALANA SHOW there in the mid-1990's. During this time they all experienced slight disturbances ranging from thumping or banging noises from the catwalk high above the sound stage which could not be explained, to some staff actually seeing specters.

In 1996 the studio took the stories seriously enough to invite The Society For Paranormal Research to investigate the phenomena. They sent out two investigators Larry Motz, who has been a paranormal investigator for 30 years, and another investigator identified as Michael.

During their investigation they uncovered several entities. They saw the ghost of a young man, whom they felt did not belong to the history of the building, on the catwalk. This man wore a gray tee-shirt and jeans. He was about 27 years old with brown hair and he looked like he was dressed in 1980's clothing. The entity seemed to recognize their presence and was not intimidated by them.

In the lobby they encountered several entities which were dressed in tuxedos from the 1940's. Two men appeared to be having an argument and one of them was shot in the chest. Another man in a tuxedo hurried through the lobby and appeared greatly upset. The investigators reported receiving high electromagnetic readings in the spot where the man who was shot had fallen.

In the upper offices they encountered an entity of a pretty young woman with clipped blond hair in a slip dress. The young woman seemed to be a performer from the 1940's era and she appeared distressed. They received the impression that she might have committed suicide in the building perhaps in the early 1940's. The young woman faded away quickly. She would later be seen upon the catwalks as they continued their work.

The investigators later learned a great deal about the building which confirmed their investigation. Is the former Earl Carroll Theater haunted? It would appear that it is. The turbulence of the past several decades in Hollywood is encapsulated in that one building.

None of the entities seems threatening, however, the young man on the catwalk does appear to want his own way. His banging during the taping of the talk shows has on occasion disturbed them.

If you ever get a chance to visit the studio for a taping of a show, perhaps you, too, will glimpse these entities from yesteryear.

CHILDER'S NIGHT

"But Jesus said, Suffer the little children, and forbid them not, to come unto me: for of such is the kingdom of heaven."
Matthew 19:13

Those of us who hunt for ghost stories know that we're always looking for a good tale. British author, Chas. Sampson would know exactly what I mean. He has been collecting and chronicling the hauntings of England for years. However, Mr. Sampson went from merely writing about ghosts to actually witnessing a most unusual haunting when he went to the small English village of Potter.

Mr. Sampson later wrote that he first became aware of a traditional haunting in the area when he read a stanza from a children's song from the fifteenth century in a library which alluded to a local stream called Horsey Mere. Mr. Sampson bided his time until he had occasion to be in the area of Horsey Mere, then began collecting whatever information he could about the village, the water which was to be haunted and the legend of old.

The history of Horsey Mere would seem impossibly old to many Americans who think a nation surviving for two hundred odd years is an accomplishment. The village of Potter near the village of Putney, once called Puttenhythe (which means landing place), was once inhabited by the Romans and the Saxons long before Europeans ever knew there was an America. This was a place where ancient boats once plied the waters of the Horsey Mere, and even in ancient times the water held a mystery.

Though the village people were reluctant to talk to the stranger about their town, an old man mentioned the hauntings but was quieted by his companions. The old man did agree, however, to go fishing with Mr. Sampson they decided to go fishing the next day on Horsey Mere.

The day was June 13 and Mr. Sampson was gratified to note that it was a lovely day. White clouds did not dispel the sunshine and only a light breeze kept things cool. One could not have wanted a more lovely day for fishing or for ghost hunting.

The two men set off in a companionable manner and soon found themselves in a small islet which was overgrown and calm.

Mr. Sampson waited a bit before asking about the haunting which was supposed to take place upon the Mere.

The old man had a thick, broad accent but Mr. Sampson followed him raptly as he spoke. "Yes, there's a story about this place but you wouldn't believe it," the old man said.

Mr. Sampson reassured him that he would very much like to hear the story.

The old fellow gave Sampson a look which sized him up before he began. "Well, did ya ever hear of the Romans?"

Of course Sampson had.

"Back in that time the Romans tramped all about this land and when their babes died they brought them here and tied weights to the babe's body and dropped it in Horsey Mere. There was a lot of childers which didn't make it in those times so many a tiny body was consigned to this here water. Their bones are still down there somewhere," the old man peered reflectively into the dark waters.

"They say them childer's spirits live on in the water and haunt this place. Every year on June 13 them childers are supposed to come back and climb back out of the water. They get to play for one hour and their voices have been heard in song. It is a mercy granted the innocent that they get to live an earthly life once each year. Them that's heard the wee ones call this night Childer's Night and we all know they'll be come back soon." As the old man finished, he looked at Sampson as if to challenge him to call him a liar.

Sampson did not know what to say. He was aware that today was June 13 and he thought perhaps the old fellow had chosen that date to add spice to his story.

The old man read the suspicious look on Sampson's face and laughed scornfully. "Ha! I knew you'd not be after believing me. Don't make me no never mind, though. I knows the story is true."

"Have you ever seen or heard the children? Has anyone else?" Sampson found himself being drawn into the story despite his cautious approach.

The old fellow nodded. "There's been two times. The first time I was a young man and the other time was only five years ago." The old fellow told his story of hearing the voices and seeing the children dancing and playing on the water's bank.

Sampson and the old man fished for a while longer before they went to visit a local inn nearby. There they met a local historian who confirmed the old man's story. The three men got along well and Sampson invited the historian to go fishing with them again that night.

Around 9:30 p.m. the three men met at the inn where they purchased food for their fishing adventure. They climbed aboard the dinghy, but then the old man insisted that they wait aboard the tiny boat which he had not untied from it's mooring line until after 1 a.m. Sampson knew immediately why the old man did not want to start out yet. They began telling tales but they did not imbibe in alcohol at all despite the fact that they had brought some with them. Sampson had determined that if anything should happen he would be stone cold sober when he witnessed it.

The night grew late and the moon scudded in and out behind clouds. About a quarter till twelve they turned off their lantern to conserve fuel and so as not to attract attention to themselves.

A gentle silence fell among the men as they enjoyed the night and nature's call. A breeze blew gently and suddenly Sampson became aware of something stirring within the wind. A sound of music, faint at first but growing louder, reached his ears. It was the most beautiful sound man could imagine and it brought Sampson to a point of awe.

As the men listened to the music, a sudden brightness grew in the depths of the water. Suddenly there was light deep in the water which shimmered upward in millions of pinpoints and the very water seemed to be moving, swaying, shifting outward. Sampson looked about in bewilderment and realized that there was no water beneath the boat though it still floated at about the same height as before. Now, though, the boat rested on air.

Around them the water was gone and the ground grew lush and verdant within seconds. The light and music grew and their attention was drawn to a bank of reeds. The reeds rustled and swayed as if a troop moved among them and the three amazed men watched as the reeds parted to reveal perfect, beautiful cherubic children who tumbled onto the water's bed which was now green grass. The children were perfectly naked and with them traveled a large lion beast astride which was a child with long golden hair.

The entire event was fantastic, yet it was unfolding before their very eyes. The children were followed by other big cats. Lions, leopards, tigers and what was surely a company of at least a thousand naked little children who laughed as they made their way along the water's bed as far as the eye could see. The men watched as the children laughed and played with the cats. They danced, sang, ran and jumped around in perfect joy. It seemed to Sampson like he was watching a scene from a Bible story where Heaven was a perfect place. Here these children had found a heavenly sanctuary of their own.

The entire scene was lit with unearthly light and yet this light was suddenly diminished by a brilliant glow which swallowed up the darkness. This brilliant light appeared amidst the children and the children were literally glowing with light now. They seemed happy to see the dazzling light and ran toward it. As they reached it, Sampson was amazed to see a man in the midst of the light. The man had long brown hair and was wearing white robes that fell to his feet. He raised his arms to embrace the children as they laughed and played around him and Sampson could not take his eyes from this being. The man of light was truly the most beautiful creature he had ever seen.

The children danced and sang around the man who joined them in their play. The man laughed and talked and seemed at one with the children who embraced him with great love and he returned their tiny embraces with even more love. It was a scene that Sampson had not ever dared to imagine, yet it was now before his hungry eyes.

The man in the light made his way among the children and cats having a kind word, a caress, a touch or a smile for each in turn. At one point a huge tiger jumped up and tried to lick the man who smiled and gently spoke to the beast which immediately obeyed.

Then the man turned toward the watchers in the boat and smiled gently at them. The look in his eyes was pure love and Sampson had never felt such joy. He would later write that there are no earthly words to describe the feeling of total love that embraced their very souls as the man gently gazed upon them.

The man of light shifted his gaze from the watchers as a tiny girl with blond curls drew his attention away. He stooped to pick her up, and as he held the child tenderly Sampson's eyes fell upon a sight that nearly stole his breath. There were wounds upon His hands. The wounds were just as seen so many times in pictures and Sampson knew with sudden unshakable certainty that they were watching Him, the man who had promised paradise to a thief. That man was now with the children in their own paradise that night. Though no one spoke, they all felt the same instant conviction as to the identity of this being who was a man but was so much more!

The watchers gradually became aware that the darkness was creeping back in. The light began to fade and the music grew distant once more. The children and beasts grew to be no more than pinpoints of light as did the being of light. Within a brief few moments the men aboard the dingy were once more afloat in the water and all seemed as it had been only a brief hour earlier.

No one dared speak, yet they knew that the others shared their thoughts. What words could they speak to tell each other of their great joy and awe at witnessing the past event?

The old man re-lit the lantern and they turned back to the shore. They took with them their liquor still untouched and their meal uneaten. Mundane human needs and wants were not able to intrude upon their vision.

Did Mr. Sampson share a delusion with the other two men aboard the boat? Did they witness something because they believed that they would? If they did, then others have shared the delusion or vision as well. In 1709 Mr. Justice Truby wrote of the same event in the December notes from the East Anglian Archaeological Society. He described the event and stated that the local folks knew well of the event but did not talk of it for fear they would frighten away the children and cost them their only earthly refuge.

Furthermore, in a volume entitled *Strange Happenings*, Townshend wrote of the same event in 1692. Could it be that some folklore comes from true events? If so, then I truly hope that Sampson's vision is true. Such a story is uncommon in the history of this world which could well use more peaceful and hopeful events.

There seems no doubt that the story of Horsey Mere and childer's Night has been known for nearly a millennium for it was written of in the verse Chas. Sampson unearthed long ago in a library which went like this:

> "Com with me to Happie-Towne
> Where lyfe is bryte and gaye,
> And little children playe all daye
> And never knowe a frowne.
> Oh, com with me and joyne them
> In theyre gladde joyous throng,
> Oh, com oute here
> To Horseye Mere
> And synge the children's songe!"
>
> Lines from "The Children's Paradise" 1460
> Anonymous

I must admonish the reader that if he ever can find a copy of the book, GHOSTS OF THE BROADS, he should read this story as Chas. Sampson originally told it. There is no way that anyone can retell the story as well as he told it. I did try to do my best to express his feelings though, because I could not bear to see this wonderful and unusual story pass into history virtually unnoticed. Perhaps others will find other mentions of it in historical documents in order to complete the picture Mr. Sampson painted so very well.

BIBLIOGRAPHY

1) **THE HAUNTED VAN BUREN INN**
   Sources: First-hand accounts from Jackie Hernandez

2) **SHARON TATE'S GHOSTLY WARNING:**
   Sources: *Helter Skelter* by Vincent Bugliosi, *Haunted Hollywood, A Ghostly Tour of Hollywood* by Laurie Jacobson, *Hauntings Across America* (T.V. documentary), *The National Directory Haunted Places* by Dennis William Hauck

3) **THE SPIRITS OF QUARANTINE STATION, AUSTRALIA**
   Sources: Australian Ghost Hunters Society, Quarantine Station staff, and TheCastle of Spirits website

4) **THE GHOSTLY KITTEN:**
   Sources: *Strange Unsolved Mysteries* by Margaret Ronan & The French Society For Psychical Research Archives

5) **LEIGH MASTERS AND SAM:**
   Source: *Haunted Adams And Other Counties* by Sally M. Barach

6) **THE CRESCENT HOTEL:**
   Sources: Packet prepared by the management, *Points* (1901), *The Flashpoint*, Eureka Springs Historical Museum, June Westphal (author & historian), *Eureka Springs Times-Echo Newspaper*, personal correspondence

7) **THE PATROL:**
   Sources: First-hand account by Mr. Prindle.

8) **THE HAUNTINGS AT HEATHROW:**
   Sources: *The Encyclopedia Of Ghosts And Spirits* by Rosemary Ellen Guiley, *MYSTERIES OF MIND SPACE & TIME*, *THE UNEXPLAINED*

9) **THE CURSE ABOARD THE TITANIC:**
   Sources: A& E Documentaries, *Eerie Tales* by Alex Hamer

10) **STONE COLD SPIRITS:**
    Sources: *The Ghosts of Richmond* by L.B. Taylor, Jr., Smithsonian National Museum of American Art the Registrar's Office, *Philadelphia Ghost Stories* by Charles J. Adams III, *GHOSTS OF THE PRAIRIE MAGAZINE*, Issue 2, Summer 1997 Troy Taylor, *National Directory of Haunted Places* by Dennis William Hauck, *Strange Unsolved Mysteries* by Margaret Ronan

11) **THE RED GIRL OF HUNTINGTON COLLEGE:**
    Sources: *Haunted Places*--Internet (theshadowlands.net), *The National Directory Haunted Places* by Dennis William Hauck

12) **WHAT WILL HAPPEN TO PHYLLIS PARKER?**
    Sources: *National Directory Haunted Places* by Dennis William Hauck, *"Phyllis--The Library Ghost"* by Eileen Luz Johnston & written correspondence with Mrs. Johnston, *The New York Times*, Sunday, Oct. 26, 1997 article *No Rest For The Eerie*

13) **BLACK JAKE AND THE DELTA SALOON:**
    Sources: *FATE Magazine* (April 1998 issue, article: *The FATE Vacation Guide To Paranormal Places*) *National Directory Haunted Places* by Dennis William Hauck

14) **HAUNTED SUNNYLAND:**
    Sources: *Haunted Places*--Internet (theshadowlands.net)

15) **THE SOUNDS FROM HELL**
    Sources: account from the family this happened to.

16) **THE MANSIONS HOTEL:**
    Sources: *Rooms With A Boo* (article) by Barbara Rose Brooker, *Strains* (article) by Zahid Sardar, personal letters to the hotel, *The National Directory Haunted Places* by Dennis William Hauck, *Haunted Houses Of California* by Antoinette May, Information provided by the management.

BIBLIOGRAPHY

17) **THE HOBO:**
Source: Second Hand account from a minister who's mother-in-law this happened to.

18) **FROM BEYOND THE GRAVE:**
Sources: *Encyclopedia Of Ghosts And Spirits* by Rosemary Ellen Guiley, *Evidence Of Life After Death* by Arthur S. Berger

19) **THE GHOSTLY CHILDREN OF SAN ANTONIO:**
Sources: *Mysteries, Magic & Miracles* (television series) and *National Directory Haunted Places* by Dennis William Hauck

20) **THE CRYING GIRL:**
Source: letters and corrospondence with the family involved.

21) **"PLAY FOR ME, BETH."**
Sources: *A Virginia Halloween: Centuries Of Scary Sightings*, Abindon Visitors Bureau.

22) **THE HAUNTINGS AT BERLIN'S OLD PALACE:**
Sources: *50 Great Ghost Stories* edited by John Canning (story by Michael and Mollie Hardwick)

23) **THE HAUNTED HIGH SCHOOL OF TIJUANA:**
Sources: *Haunted Places*--Internet (theshadowlands.net)

24) **THE MANSION CALLED FAIRACRES:**
"The Gallery of Ghosts: The eerie and unexplained in old Burnaby Mansion by John Armstrong for *Vancouver Sun*, Oct. 31, 1987, *Historic Haunted America* by Michael Norman & Beth Scott

25) **THE HAUNTED OPRAH WINFREY STUDIO:**
Sources: Oprah Winfrey Show tape, Chicago Historical Society records, Richard T. Crowe of Chicago Supernatural Tours in phone conversation and through correspondence, *National Enquirer* article *Oprah's Show Is Haunted* by John South and Denny Johnson (June 29, 1993)

26) **ABRAHAM LINCOLN AND THE RATHBONE CURSE:**
Sources: *The Haunted Major* by Gene Smith, *American Heritage* Feb./March 1994, *Under The Shadow Of Lincoln's Murder* by Mary Joe Clendenin (internet *A Word Edgewise-*), *Union College Magazine* (article 9) *Henry and Clara*, by Erika Mancini

27) **THE GHOST OF GILLAN'S WAY:**
Sources: *Mysteries Of Mind, Space & Time* book 11 *The Unexplained Turning In His Grave* (article) by Frank Smyth

28) **THE BEST LITTLE RESTAURANT:**
Source: First-hand account sent to me in a letter, *Mysteries Of Mind, Space & Time* book 6 *The Unexplained*, first-person account and corrospondence with some of those involved.

29) **THE LAST GOOD-BYE:**
Sources: First hand account and corrospondence by Carl W. Sypolt.

30) **NELLY BUTLER'S RETURN:**
Sources: *Prominent American Ghosts* by Susy Smith

31) **THE VOICES:**
Sources: Letters from people who have had similar experiences with disembodied voices.

32) **THE WILLOW SALOON:**
Sources: *Sightings* (television series), *National Directory Haunted Places* by Dennis William Hauck

33) **THE HAUNTED STUDIO:**
HAUNTINGS TODAY NEWSLETTER by Larry Montz, parapsychologist from internet source (http://www.neworleans.com/hauntings/newsletter.html)

34) **CHILDER'S NIGHT:**
Sources: *Ghosts Of The Boards* by Chas. Sampson

If you have enjoyed this book then you are invited to purchase autographed copies of Patty A. Wilson's other books:

HAUNTED PENNSYLVANIA:
List Price: $16.95
Order Number 001

In author Patty A. Wilson's first book you will discover the unknown byways and hidden haunts of Pennsylvania.
- Visit Elmhurst estate where a Gibson girl still walks.
- Read about the Ghost Ships of Lake Erie and the old hag of Rt. 22.
- Learn what happened in Gettysburg during the filming of the movie.
- Read about the Jean Bonnet Tavern's half dozen dead residents.
- Take a journey on an unknown part of Pennsylvania history and delight in the thrills and shivers this book evokes.

THE PENNSYLVANIA GHOST GUIDE VOL. I
List Price: $14.95
Order Number 002

Ms. Wilson takes you on a guided fright ride through Pennsylvania's most haunted spots including the ghosts of:
- Penn State's many campuses
- A haunted antique store that was once a whore house
- Dickinson College's spirit students
- Meet a Native American spirit who lives with and protects a woman in Ja-Jubba
- Learn about the ghosts in Gettysburg--including a personal tale
- Read about a dead Pope who appeared to two trapped men and stayed with them for 10 days.
- pp. 154 includes 26 authentic photos

THE PENNSYLVANIA GHOST GUIDE VOL. II
List Price: $14.95
Order Number 003

Ms. Wilson offers up over thirty more true stories from Pennsylvania's paranormal history.
- Visit the U.S. Hotel in Hollidaysburg that is perhaps the most haunted site in the state!
- Learn about a child who grew up in a haunted house in Brownsville and who, to this day, deals with that entity.
- Visit the Fulton Opera House where the spirits still tread the boards and horrible acts mar the history of this beautiful site.
- Read about hauntings from Pittsburgh to Philadelphia and be surprised by how many of the stories were never told before.
- pp. 125 29 authentic photos

THE PARANORMAL PERSPECTIVE
JOURNAL OF THE PARANORMAL RESEARCH FOUNDATION
Subscription price: $20 per year
Order Number 004

This organization that was created by Patty A. Wilson, Scott Crownover and Al Brindza is dedicated to using the scientific method to validate or debunk ghosts and hauntings. Each month you will receive a journal (approx. 20 pages) filled with valuable information about ghost hunting. Follow current investigations, ask questions or even join the group if you'd like.

Send checks or money orders along with the name of each book ordered, the order number and the quantity to:

Piney Creek Press
PO Box 227
Roaring Spring, PA 16673
Allow 3-4 weeks for delivery.

PA Residents please add 6% sales tax
Add $2. shipping for the first book and
$1 for each additional book.

Thank You